waiting for the fall

coming home.
following Christ.

maggie jordan

the events documented in this work represent the author's memories and perspective. it is acknowledged and understood that the same events and memories are subjective and may be interpreted, understood, and remembered differently from another's perspective.

this work is not an official publication of the Church of Jesus Christ of Latter-day Saints. the author does not claim to represent the church nor does her work provide any sort of authoritative or representative position for the church. the purpose of this work is to express the author's views, experiences, and opinions.

cover art credit :: © Jacqueline Merrill 2020
back cover photo credit :: Jazlynn Steed 2020

editor credit :: Rachel Bird
formatting and cover design credit :: Shelley Sonderegger

ISBN :: (paperback) 978-1-7348761-0-9
(ebook) 978-1-7348761-1-6

Library of Congress Control Number :: 2020907194

Ogden, Utah, USA
independently published

nakedsoullife.org

attn :: la Petien

me cambiaste la vida che.
y no sería la persona que soy sin haberte conocido.

a mi familia ::
por su amor incondicional.
y por apoyarme en mis sueños de ser escritora.

a mis queridos uruguayos ::
les amo. les extraño.
y siguen en mis oraciones siempre.

a Presidente y Hermana Smith
y a mis diez compañeras tan queridas ::

son mi familia eterna del corazón.
y el impacto que tuvieron en mi vida no tiene comparación.

y a los élderes y las hermanas de la misión Uruguay Montevideo Oeste (2013-2015)

hoy es el día.

vívalo.

0 ::

I've been home five years now.

five years.

and sometimes it still feels like yesterday.

I served a full-time service mission for the church of Jesus Christ of Latter-day Saints.

in Uruguay.

it's below Brazil and next to Argentina if you didn't know. national language is Spanish. and I loved it. I love that country. it became my home. it's still my second home. I love the culture. and the people. and the eighteen months I spent there. most of all, I loved the person I became while I was there.

and coming home from that was one of the most difficult and painful experiences of my life up until that point.

looking back, I knew nothing. nothing about what it would be like to come home. I mean I guessed there would be some heartache and discomfort trying to figure out what I was doing afterward. but I really didn't know. it's just one of those things you can't really understand or explain until you've been through it.

so I'm just here to talk about it. because I've been there. and I've felt it.

five years ago . . . that was hell for me. coming home was so hard. harder than leaving my family to serve the mission. harder than my worst days out there. coming home was awful. and I fell apart. to be honest. there was very little anyone else could do or say to help me through it. I felt helpless. unsure about my future. and confused about my next steps. I didn't know what to do.

so I did what I do know how to do.

I wrote.

and I kept writing.

and what you have in your hands now is the result :: raw, honest feelings. experiences. struggles. and truths.

this is my story.

this is the path I walked after coming home.

it's different from yours. but it can still help you. you can learn from my story. and I can learn from yours. we're going to the same destination. just taking different paths to get there.

and we can do this together. because pain is universal. grief is universal. sorrow is universal. but so are growth. and peace. and joy.

some people come home from the mission and don't even miss a step. their path is clear. with very few setbacks. they seem to transition easily. naturally. and then walk right into the next stage of their lives.

other people (like me) walk into glass walls literally everywhere and couldn't stay on their feet if someone paid them to. our path is less clear. with more setbacks. and the transition is not easy or natural. and we end up getting dumped into the next stage of life unwillingly.

and as for everybody else. well, they're all somewhere in the middle.

the point is, you do not have to walk alone. doesn't matter what path you're on. because we're all going to the same destination ::

eternal life. through the atoning, saving power of Jesus Christ.

He is the Son of God. He is our Brother. He is the Savior of you. and He is the Savior of me. He felt every pain. and sacrificed Himself for every single person who has been or ever will be born to this earth. He walked your path. and He walked mine. and He walked alone so that you and I would never have to.

that's what I want you to take from this book. more than anything else. that He is here for you. and that never changes.

our God is a God who loves His people.

and our Savior is a Savior who walks with His people.

He is with you on your path. post-mission path. recently-baptized path. or any path really. He knows the way. and He wants you to follow Him so He can show you the way.

following Christ = discipleship

put simply.

disciples of Jesus Christ = people who love and follow Him

and that's all of us. anyone who follows Christ.

but listen. as a full-time missionary, your role was different. you didn't just follow Christ. you actually represented Him. you chose to be called and set apart from others and given the responsibility to represent Him and help people come to Him.

that c h a n g e d you.

and in order to move forward down your path successfully, you have to know that.

you are not the same person you were before you left your home. because sacred experiences with God change us. especially extended ones like serving a mission.

you learned how to follow Him.

that's what the mission teaches you. that's what being a part of the church of Jesus Christ of Latter-day Saints teaches us.

and I firmly believe that there is one singular, most critical life-guiding question you n e e d to know how to answer. over and over again. regularly. consistently. without fail. every single day.

what are you willing to give to follow Jesus Christ?

who are you willing to become? what are you willing to sacrifice? how willing are you to listen to Him? and ultimately do what it takes to follow Him? today. tomorrow. for the rest of your life.

because He is the reason.

the reason we came to earth. the reason we're baptized. the reason we serve missions. the reason we do our best to lives good lives and be good people. the reason we can be forgiven for our mistakes and be right with God. over and over again.

because without Him, we have nothing. we are nothing. we can become nothing. and we could never make it home to the presence of God, our Heavenly Father again after this life. it all points back to Him. and His selfless sacrifice. He died so that we could live again.

if we truly believe that He is the reason, following Him comes naturally.

and this is true for all disciples of Jesus Christ. not just for returned missionaries. but to each and every baptized person in the church of Jesus Christ of Latter-day Saints. and to any others who follow Him.

following Him should be our number one priority.

and that's what I want you to get from this book. regardless of your experience coming home. whether you did a tuck-and-roll and kept running off the plane or whether you crash-landed and fell apart.

the only thing that makes anything we do worth anything is whether or not we are actively choosing to follow Jesus Christ.

so let's get into it.

1 ::

serving a mission is kind of like climbing a tree.

not really.

but kind of.

think about climbing a tree. or riding a bike. or diving into a pool. they all have something in common :: if you have ever unsuccessfully performed one of the above activities, you've met gravity firsthand.

now think about gravity. I can guarantee that thanks to gravity, we've all fallen. at one point or another. it is a law of nature. gravity cannot change. so in order to avoid falling

w e c h a n g e

for our safety mostly. gravity teaches us respect. caution. fear. mastery. among other things.

after we fall the first time, we learn to expect it. after any heightening experience. we know that what goes up must definitely come back down. and in order to survive, we just accept that truth. and we learn to respect gravity.

now if we respect gravity, we won't try to defy it unprepared. like climbing a tall tree without a harness. or riding a bike on the freeway without a helmet. knowing we could fall makes us more cautious. because we don't want to get hurt.

with that knowledge we can either fear or master gravity. fear says don't climb the tree because you might fall. mastery says wear a harness so you don't fall and die. fear says don't jump off the diving board. mastery says make sure the water is deep enough and learn how to dive so you don't paralyze yourself.

do you see the difference? fear limits. mastery empowers.

because the truth is that f a l l i n g i s i n e v i t a b l e .

so we can either wait in fear for it to happen. or we can learn to master it.

we have that choice.

when we wait for the fall, we freeze up. we panic. we don't prepare. and we end up getting hurt.

falling over and over again without changing our methods teaches us an unnecessary fear of heights. avoiding heights for fear of falling decreases our quality of life. and waiting for the fall just postpones living.

that's not the way life was meant to be lived.

which means our only real option is to master the ability to fall safely. and mastery takes time.

when we choose to master the ability to fall, we take risks and we learn. and we change. mastery does not come without failed attempts. and learning from those failed attempts helps us grow.

so let's talk about a less physical kind of fall.

because serving a mission is kind of like climbing a tree.

not really.

but kind of.

it's a spiritual tree.

you learn so much from serving a mission. about God. Jesus Christ. the principles of His gospel. you give your time and heart and effort and your whole self to serve Him. and to serve the people around you. every single day. you are a literal representative of Jesus Christ.

and then one day you step off the plane. the name tag is removed from your chest. and it's all over. just. like. that.

you fall out of the tree. essentially.

when I came home, I fell. and I didn't just fall.

nope.

I crash-landed. face in the dirt. broken to pieces. no harness. no safety net. no helmet. nothing. I crashed. I didn't know what to do. or where to go. unable to process what had just happened. I was numb. and I fell apart. completely.

coming home was the literal worst. and I had to explain to my family over and over again that no, I did not hate them. that yes, I did miss them while I was gone. but that no, I did not want to be at home. and that no, it wasn't their fault.

I felt lonely. confused. depressed. lost. I wanted to go back to the mission. back to what I had. back to serving God every day. to feeling needed. and important. but it doesn't work that way.

not every day was like that when I came home. some days were happier. there were days when things felt okay. peaceful. calm. I felt loved. and wanted. and more stable. but those were not as common for me for at least six months after coming home.

and it was so hard.

everyone falls after coming home from the mission.

it's inevitable.

we all fall out of that spiritual tree. and it's not because we did something wrong. it's because we aren't supposed to live there. we're not birds. we're people. we climb trees and mountains and overcome obstacles to push ourselves. to learn. to see the view. and then we come back down. and we go on to find more trees or mountains or obstacles to overcome.

we go up. and then we come back down.

some people fall gracefully. they land on their feet and head off to the next tree. others hit literally every branch on the way down and end up on the ground in a broken mess. that was me. and maybe that was you too.

whatever your experience was, you fell. and it might have been the first time you fell spiritually like that. and it hurt.

but there's something you have to know and trust ::

God knew you would fall.
and it's going to be okay.

I promise you He knew. and He knew it would be hard. how could it not be hard? and how could He not know?

the literal Fall of mankind came before the Atonement of Jesus Christ took place. the fall came before the healing. that was true then. and it is true now with you and me.

i t i s u n r e a l i s t i c

to think that a young man or woman could be in the service of God for an extended period of their life and expect to come home the same person. unchanged. unaffected by what they had just lived. after serving God for every single moment of every single day for eighteen months or two years or however long you served for. you changed. I know I did. that's just what happens.

God knew we would fall. but He never meant for us to fall alone. and He meant for us to stand back up and climb those spiritual trees again.

because He loves us.

and He knows us.

God is our Father. our literal Father. and He sent His Son. our literal Brother. to suffer and bleed and die for us so that we never have to go through anything alone. and that includes coming home from the mission.

so then the choice is ours. we can choose to wait for the fall. or we can choose to master it and start climbing again.

let me explain ::

to wait for the fall after coming home from a mission is to stop living big spiritually for no good reason other than the fact that you fell.

and that's not okay.

it's a choice to come home and to stop actively climbing those spiritual trees. it comes from fear. and pain. maybe some annoyance. probably pride too. and it's holding you back. big time.

it's like deciding to never ride a bike again because you fell off. or refusing to dive again because you belly-flopped. it's a choice you're making that's stopping you from living.

waiting for the fall after coming home shows a lack of interest in running your spiritual life. it happens when you stop making meaningful decisions with God's help. when you revert back to your old habits. when you forget the patterns of conversion you learned. when you let hopelessness and despair take over. when you believe you are useless and abandoned. and you distance yourself from God. when you lose your sense of spiritual direction. and let the world pull you wherever it would. or worse, when go back to being the exact same person you were before you left.

let me be clear :: I am not talking about sin. we all sin. and we all make mistakes. and we repent. and we grow again. this is different.

waiting for the fall to break you is a decision. a decision to stop seeking out God and to stop making Him a priority after promising to follow Him forever. and it's a mistake.

yet so often, that is what we do when we come home from missions. we wait for that fall. because we've been told to. or because we don't know any better. or because don't allow ourselves to expect anything better or more of ourselves.

but do you really think that's how God intended for it to be? for us to come home and fall apart and give up our discipleship?

God doesn't kick us out of the tree.

that's a lie.

yes. a lie.

and it is one of satan's finest.

I'm going to tell you something special. sacred. and near to my heart. life altering. conversion steadying. sanctifying. and truly glorious. something that changed my post-mission experience and taught me an eternal lesson. I'm going to tell you the way God intended for it to be.

you were not meant to fall apart.

read it again.

you were not meant to fall apart .

to fall is not a choice.

but to fall apart when you hit the ground is.

I'd heard about how hard it was to come home from serving a mission. to come home and lose your mission spirit. to lose that closeness to God. to feel less of His presence and to go back to being just another person who half-heartedly goes to church. sure sounded like getting kicked out of the tree to me.

and it seemed like everybody knew it was going to happen. like it was some natural, expected thing to just come home and get kicked out of the tree. my family knew it. my friends knew it. other returned missionaries warned me of it. satan was more than ready and willing to remind me of it every. single. day.

they made it seem so natural as if even God Himself was in on it. and that terrified me.

but I didn't want to believe it.

because that was not like my God.

my God who I loved and served. my God who knew me and loved me. He wouldn't just push me out of the tree because my time in the mission was done.

but instead of trusting that, I panicked. I waited for the fall to happen and then I let it happen. I let fear take over. and pride too. I felt like God just kicked me out of the spiritual tree I climbed with Him. I crash-landed and fell apart. and it hurt. so, so much.

and I honestly believe the only reason that this was my experience coming home was so that I could sit down and write this book and testify to you that you do not have to fall apart.

you can master this fall.

because just like with everything else in this life, to fall is not a choice. we don't get to choose whether or not gravity exists. we don't get to choose whether or not our mission ends. but we do get to choose whether we will wait for the fall to come or master it. whether we will get back up. or crumble apart. come out stronger. or give up. continue being disciples. or stop.

because here's the truth ::

there is no instinctual, knee-jerk, reflex-type chemical reaction between returning home from a mission and falling into a spiritual apostasy. you essentially gave yourself to God. and that means something to Him. and it should mean something to you.

the mission wasn't meant to be some spiritual high that was just supposed to end the day you came home. throwing you into a wall of depressed numbness and pain with a hangover that would last for a few days, months, weeks, or possibly even years.

it wasn't meant to be a spiritual launch pad either. from dedicated discipleship into a lawless, unguided world where you get to choose your level of dedication to Christ.

coming home wasn't some alarm clock that woke you up to tell you your nice spiritual experience was over and it was time to get back to the real world to start your mediocre adult life.

it wasn't meant to be a walk of shame away from following Christ because your time ran out.

coming home is not comparable to Lot's wife in the Bible, who was cursed and turned into a pillar of salt just for looking back on her previous life after God commanded her not to (*The Bible,* Genesis 19:26).

coming home from a mission is not the same.

when we incorrectly view the end of a mission as a fall from grace or a fall from God. as a stage we passed through or a box we checked. we miss the point. and if that's where you're at, you missed it. if it was easy to come home and toss your missionary experience aside, you missed it.

"well done, thou good and faithful servant" (*The Bible,* Matthew 25:21) is not a welcome home sign in the airport. it is not a pat on the back and a send off from spirituality into your adult life.

it will be an invitation from God Himself to enter into His presence in the next life.

and that's it.

you sacrificed a portion of your life to be set apart as a full-time missionary for the church of Jesus Christ of Latter-day Saints to serve God. and even if it was the most difficult, awful experience of your life, it was still meant to sanctify you. to bring you to God. to change you.

p e r m a n e n t l y .

and there is no way that doesn't mean something to Him.

He spent so much time teaching us. the mission is a sacred, refining training. and it's freaking hard. it tests your faith and diligence. teaches you how to pray and speak to God. to connect with him on a deeper level. and it makes me sad to think that after so much dedication and commitment and time and effort. after so much growth and change :: that it could all be undone.

as a missionary you were given a c a l l i n g to teach you d i s c i p l e s h i p .

when you came home, you were released from the c a l l i n g .
but not the d i s c i p l e s h i p .

so when we come home. and the calling ends. and we mistakenly think discipleship ended too. we miss the point. of all of it.

that's what I mean by waiting for the fall. and by falling apart.

your sacrifice was not meaningless. and your discipleship did not end when they took that name tag off your chest. you were not meant to fall apart.

nope.

so you have to learn how to master the fall. you just have to.

and the way to do that is through discipleship.

discipleship isn't a one-time thing. as Elder Dieter F. Uchtdorf said, "discipleship is not a spectator sport" (Uchtdorf, 2009). when you committed to follow Christ, it was for life. not for eighteen months. or two years. or for however long you served. that's the reason why we all came to this life to begin with. to follow Christ. it's such a vital part of who we are. and the mission is just one of the many experiences that can remind us of that and teach us how to follow Him.

let me explain.

I love soccer. you can play soccer anywhere. sure, it's nice to play on a clean turf field, but you can play on a cement basketball court or a dirt field just as easily. all you need is a ball and other people. as long as you know how to play, you can play anywhere. because how you play matters more than where you play. simple.

apply that to discipleship. how you live the gospel matters more than where you live it. if you know how, you can live it anywhere. you need Christ. and His gospel. and a desire to follow Him. that's it. simple.

you and I followed Christ before this life. and we followed Him in the mission. and we can follow Him here and now just the same. because how you follow Him matters more than where you follow Him.

it's like leaving the missionary training center and going to your actual mission field. you went to a foreign environment but you carried with you all the same tools and principles you had before. the same goals and testimonies. all you needed was Christ and a desire to follow Him. and you changed and developed a more appropriate lifestyle to fit the new circumstances.

the exact same concept applies to post mission life. you brought home with you the same tools and principles you had there. the same goals and testimonies. and even more experience. now you're just on a different playing field. and it's time to develop a more appropriate lifestyle to fit the circumstances.

so think about where you're at. did you crash-land? did you come home and check a box? did you put it all behind you? did you let it change you?

wherever you're at is between you and God. He knows you and He is with you.

I crashed because I thought my discipleship had ended. and I failed to realize that the only thing that had changed was my calling.

so coming home, should your level of commitment to the Lord change?

no.

because discipleship is not a sprint. it's a marathon. and the mission was just a warm-up lap.

you were not called to serve just so God could show you what discipleship looked like should you c h o o s e to follow Christ.

no.

you were being reminded of why you came to earth to begin with. to f o l l o w Christ.

He didn't just teach you discipleship. He molded you into a disciple. and that molding was intended to be for life. for the rest of your life.

so don't fall away. don't get lost. don't give up. and if you do, come back. a guilty conscience is your soul's way of reminding you. reminding you of who you are. reminding you that you can change and repent and grow.

so listen to it.

don't wait to come home and fall apart. don't expect it. and don't let yourself believe that coming home will break you. will it be hard? umm yeah. but honestly, the best things are.

when you do fall, get back up. realize that falling is a normal part of life. choose to keep following our Savior. that's what I did and what I keep trying to do. and so can you.

now I am not saying that we're supposed to dedicate all of our time and energy to God. that is the job of a full-time missionary. that's not the job of a disciple of Christ. we have to work, go to school, get married, raise families :: our responsibilities have changed. but our commitment has to stay the same. centered in Christ.

we're supposed to enjoy this life. and that enjoyment is supposed to go hand in hand with following Christ. it is made whole and full and complete through Him. two of my favorite scriptures really sum up why we're here. at least for me they do ::

Christ speaking :: "and he said unto the children of men, 'follow thou me'" (*The Book of Mormon,* 2 Nephi 31:10).

talking about us :: "Adam fell that men might be; and men are that they might have joy" (*The Book of Mormon,* 2 Nephi 2:25).

that is why we're here.

to follow Christ. and to have joy.

and honestly when it comes down to it, that's it. if following Christ is our number one priority, we will be happy.

He wants us to be as happy as we possibly can be.

and He knows that the happiest we'll ever be is by doing what we came here to do :: by following Christ.
French philosopher Pierre Teilhard de Chardin said that "we are not human beings having a spiritual experience. we are spiritual beings having a human experience." and I love that.

we are children of a God who loves us.

we are eternal beings.

our potential is limitless and incredible.

He made us strong.

not so that we would never fall. but so that we would not fall apart.

and so that we would rise again through Him. that strength comes from within. from eternities of preparation. from our Father. and our ability to follow Christ will be a determining factor in our eternal progress on our journey home. the mission wasn't the start of that journey. it was a chance to learn discipleship and carry those changes with you for the rest of your life.

so let's talk about how to do that.

2 ::

before I left for Uruguay, I had no idea just how much the mission was going to change me. and how much God was going to change me. I changed a lot. like a full 180°. I came home a new person. and I'm so grateful I did.

I was born and raised in the church of Jesus Christ of Latter-day Saints. I was baptized when I was eight years old. I always went to church. and seminary. and institute. I could recite scriptures from memory. I knew the words to the hymns. I knew what was expected of me and I always did it. because it made me happy. but after a few days in the missionary training center. yes. days. of learning how to teach people about those same things I'd been taught my whole life, I realized that I had no idea what I was talking about.

and I didn't even know if I believed any of it.

I told myself nah you're good. you know these things. and I did know them. as facts. but when I sat down and got real with myself, I saw just how unsure I really was. about all of it.

I was blessed to be raised with the gospel of Jesus Christ. so I knew it. but I didn't feel it. I didn't understand it. and honestly I didn't care to progress in it any more. until I went on my mission.

and about three weeks into my mission on what to this day is still the loneliest, darkest night of my life, I knelt down before my Savior and asked Him to comfort me. and He did. I had never been so broken. so alone. so vulnerable. and He was there. for all of it. and He loved me still. He stayed with me. I came to know Him. and I committed to follow Him forever. to be His disciple. that sacred, quiet experience set off a chain of events and uncovered a deep desire to change that I had never felt before.

and that's when my life started to change.

those eighteen months taught me so much about God. about His nature. about myself. and about discipleship. I grew a backbone. developed opinions. learned to teach and testify. to be confident in myself and in my God. I went through hard things and overcame them. I was so happy. so content. ready to take on anything that came my way. because I knew where I stood with God.

for the first time in my life I got a sense of who I really was and of who I wanted to become.

and that was all new for me.

He changed me. and continues to change me. and I am forever grateful for Him.

I came home a different person than I was when I left. and five years later, I'm different again. I've changed. and my guess is that you've changed too. God loves us in all our stages.

but He still wants us to change.

He expects us to change.

we were not meant to stay the same. think about it. the whole reason God sent His p e r f e c t Son Jesus Christ to suffer and die for us was so that we could have the ability to repent.

repentance = sincere change

He wanted to give us the chance to c h o o s e t o c h a n g e ourselves every single day for the rest of our lives as we did our best to follow Him.

so if you changed on the mission, good for you. if you didn't as much, that's fine too. my point is that God did change you. in important, sacred ways. and those changes you made in the mission. the person you became. the closeness to God you developed. none of that was meant to end.

to shift yes. but to end no.

let me explain.

j a n u a r y 9, 2 0 1 5.

the day I got off the plane and went to the church building to be released from my calling as a full-time missionary. and up to that point in my life, it was one of the w o r s t days of my life. I didn't know what to expect. and I was pretty freaked out to be honest. I'd heard all the stories. and I'm sure you have too.

the stories about the day your name tag comes off.

I felt like they ripped my heart out.
I just couldn't feel the spirit so strongly after that.
I felt like a normal person again.
I've never felt so sad or cried so hard in my life.
it was the worst day of my life.
I felt abandoned by God.
it was over. I'd done my duty.
I did what God expected, and then it was my turn to live for me.
that's when I felt free again.
I didn't know what to do.
empty. I just felt empty.
I felt replaceable.
I felt useless.

dramatic right? but no seriously, I heard these things all the time. from family. friends. other missionaries. random people. literally anyone who had an opinion shared it and it usually sounded like one of those lines. and I hated it. it was in all my emails the weeks before I came home. it was all anybody ever had to say to me about it. and I didn't know any differently, so I figured that must just be how it felt to come home from the mission.

b u t i t d i d n o t r e s t w i t h m y s o u l .

it just didn't make sense to me. and I could not understand how a God who loved His children so much could let them go from serving Him one minute to no longer needing them the next.

go back to the tree metaphor.

God does not kick His children out of the tree.

I repeat. God does not kick His children out of the tree.

that is not in His nature. and there was no way in my mind that the God who loved me and dedicated so much time to make me His would expect me to come home and leave it all behind. it didn't make sense. and I was left with such a void. a void that didn't heal even a little for at least six months. and didn't fully heal until about three years later.

so I didn't accept it. any of it. I didn't want to believe I would feel all those things people talked about. but I also didn't know what to expect. so I froze up. and I waited for the fall. just hoping I would finally understand and be strong enough to pick myself up after.

thinking about taking my name tag off terrified me. because I loved my mission. it was so freaking hard. every single day. but it was also so beautiful. and I loved it. I loved the person I became. because I became His.

I didn't want the way God spoke to me to change. I didn't want to stop serving Him and other people. I didn't want to lose that closeness to Him. or lose the sound of His voice. or not feel Him in my life every day.

and that's when I realized I didn't want anything to change. I decided I'd changed enough. I liked the way I was changing on the mission. and coming home was a change I didn't even want to think about. needless to say I was completely unprepared when I came home.

so I walked into the church building that night with my parents just waiting for the fall. my stake president thanked me for my service and asked my mom to take my name tag off. she did so very carefully and respectfully. set it into my open hands and for a second I just sat there.

waiting.

waiting to be kicked out of the tree. waiting for the fall. waiting to feel crushed. waiting for all of those awful horror stories to come true.

but nothing happened.

and the horror stories didn't happen.

and I felt hope start to grow inside as I realized that maybe. just maybe. none of it was true.

my stake president continued the interview. he and my dad gave me a blessing. and then I went home with my parents.

and still nothing happened.

days passed. weeks passed. months passed. and now five years later I can stand here and tell you that the fall didn't break me. and it doesn't have to break you either. now don't get me wrong. coming home was literally one of the worst things I've ever had to go through. I fell and fell apart and had to pick myself up and go again. it took time. and it was so hard. and I hated it.

but it was not the day that God turned His back on me.

it was not the day He decided He no longer needed me or loved me. it was not the start of the end. it was a shift. nothing more than a hard and painful shift.

but it was not an impossible one.

because He was there. I had given eighteen months of my life to Him. and when I needed Him the most, He was by my side. He helped me heal.

I know what it feels like to come home from the best, most spiritual time of your life and have it taken away from you in less than ten minutes.

I know what it feels like to be a leader :: needed and special and experienced and impactful one day. with a clear-cut purpose every morning when you wake up. and to come home lost, disoriented, and feel completely useless the very next day.

coming home from serving a mission is a complete life shift that feels like it was against your will but yet somehow you agreed to it.

I get it.

there were days when I sat in my bed or on the bathroom floor or in my car and just cried. I wanted to go back to the mission. to feel needed and useful. to feel like God was relying on me the same way He did while I was serving Him. and I just didn't. I felt His love. but I wanted more. I wanted what I had before.

and then there were days when I woke up feeling just fine. I started another semester of college. went to church and made friends. I got a few jobs. and I felt like I was making progress.

then I'd wake up sad and frustrated and upset in the morning just hurting. wanting to go back. and then two hours later I'd feel fine. or vice versa. I would wake up feeling great and then compare it to the mission and cry. because it just hurt. and I knew that something was missing.

I remember being so time-conscious. feeling like I was wasting my time if I wasn't actively doing something at every minute of every day. I felt guilty if I didn't read my scriptures. I felt guilty if I didn't share the gospel with everyone or talk about church throughout the day. I just felt guilty.

I'm pretty sure I ran through every single possible emotion when I came home. I'm already an emotional person. but this was just awful. it was like running full speed through a forest of low-hanging branches. yeah. pretty awful.

maybe you're running through them too.

sadness … that I didn't feel as spiritual as before.
fear … that I would never get to that point again.
betrayal … that God would let me fall and expect me to pick myself up and go again.
anger … that all my changes felt pointless and meaningless.
longing … to feel needed.
hollow … trying to fill this new void in my heart.
more fear … that I might never feel whole again.
regret … that I didn't take more chances or appreciate the mission more while I was there.
dread … that I had to explain to my loved ones why I was so upset to be home.
worry … that they wouldn't understand.
pain … when they didn't understand.
anxiety … that I didn't always have something to do.
guilt … for not always doing something.
shame … for not being a missionary anymore. even though it was no longer expected of me.

the list goes on and on. and I'm sure you have a running list too. go write it down. it helps to label what you're feeling and why. to understand that feelings come and go. and you don't have to feel them alone.

coming home from a mission is hard. so many things change.

but the nature of God is not one of those things.

your calling changes. your location. your schedule. your mindset. your focus. there is so much to think about and figure out. but whether or not God cares for you is not one of those things that changes. God is still your Father. He still loves you. you matter as much to Him now as you did then. and that love will never change. no matter what you do.

God does not abandon His children.

and when we realize that and believe that, coming home gets a little bit easier. we fall with more grace than before. and we pick ourselves up and move forward more easily.

see because your last day on the mission is really your first day home. it's just another transfer day. a transfer back into your most familiar environment :: your home. your family. your previous life. and this will be your "area" for the foreseeable future.

see, the challenge returned missionaries face coming home is not h o w to live the gospel. that's what you just did for eighteen months or two years or however long you served for. you know how to love people. you know how to teach. you know how to live the gospel you taught.

that's not the challenge.

your challenge is to continue to be a disciple. to not wait for the fall. and to not be afraid to live big spiritually.

your challenge is to keep the covenants you made. to not go back to the life you led before. to not give up or abandon what God spent so much time teaching you. to not leave behind those changes you made. to stay close to Him and learn to recognize His voice in a louder, more chaotic world. and I can guarantee that you will not be able to hear His voice the same way if you go back to your old life. even if that old life was good.

you can't go backwards and forwards at the same time. go back to your old life and you stop going forward into the future God has for you.

that's your challenge coming home.

and it's not an easy one.

serving a mission teaches you discipleship. teaches you the importance and the nature of change. and honestly my hardest fight coming home from the mission was defending and maintaining those changes God had made within me. discipleship is a lifestyle. not a calling. its something we keep actively living. those changes you made matter. they mattered to me. they should matter to you. but they don't really matter to anyone else.

and it didn't take me long to realize that. and that's not mean. it's just life.

nobody else cares.

but everyone has an opinion.

and I swear I heard it all when I came home.

I've been told I haven't grown up. haven't moved on from the mission. that it isn't healthy to still think about and miss the mission. it's immature, they said. told me I needed to put it behind me. be an adult and leave it in the past. that I have to let go if I'm going to progress. that I needed to stop trying so hard to be good. and that I would give up sooner or later. that it was time to humble myself and be a normal person again.

I hate that word :: normal.

I've been told the mission was a nice experience but that now I needed to grow up and live an adult life in the real world. ugh. real world. I hate that phrase too. I know I wasn't dreaming. and I'm pretty sure I wasn't smoking anything. so I'm pretty sure I was living. in the real world. serving God. on a mission.

I was told that those changes I'd made were just part of a stage I was going through. and that they wouldn't last. they weren't meant to last they said. they told me I needed to adjust faster and let it go. and I needed to stop acting like I had something to prove.

and that hurt.

but that's what I came home to.

and no. this is not a pity story.

it's an eye opener.

we're getting real and honest about what happens when you come home from a mission. because I know I'm not the only one who heard those things when I came home. that "friendly advice" hurt more than it helped. it was awful. to be told that the last eighteen months of my life were a "nice experience" or a "stage" I needed to let go of. that sucked. and it didn't make sense.

the people I left behind for eighteen months to go serve God were now referring to the most sacred experience of my l i f e up to that point as a phase. a stage. it annoyed me to hear those things from people I didn't know. and it broke my heart to hear them from people I did know and love.

now not everyone gave the less-than-helpful advice I talked about above.
some people were genuinely happy I'd changed. they encouraged me to keep going. they understood how special and unique the mission experience is to everyone. those people were my lights when I was struggling. they pointed me back to the Savior when I didn't know where to go or what to do.

they listened. they supported. and to those people I am so grateful.

let me tell you something important about those people around you who will welcome you home. people you've known since you were a kid. or a teenager. people who have seen you grow and change. people who expect certain behaviors of you because they "know you for who you really are." family. cousins. aunts. uncles. grandparents. friends. friends of friends. neighbors. people in the ward you know. people in the ward you don't know. random people. everyone who thinks they've just got to share their opinion.

they mean well.

I really think they do.

but that doesn't make them right.

and they could still most definitely be wrong.

because in reality, what anyone else has to say about your mission experience doesn't matter. what happened out there was between

y o u   a n d   G o d

and that's it.

there's a reason all those people didn't go with you. no matter how well they might know you, none of them know you as well as God does.

and they weren't there when He changed you.

your identity and your potential are not limited to someone else's interpretation of you. doesn't matter if they raised you. they cannot determine who you should be. that's between you and God.

so accept that you're probably going to hear it all when you come home. the good and the bad. but you definitely don't have to listen to it all. that's too overwhelming. so see the good in what they say and move along.

when I came home, I started going to the young single adult ward. and a few months in I met with my bishop. I don't even remember what we were arguing about or why we were arguing to begin with. but at one point he sat back in his chair, folded his arms, and gave me the most annoyed sigh I'd heard in a while. and then he told me something I'd never forget.

he told me my greatest and worst qualities were the same thing :: I was unreasonably stubborn.

and I laughed. which I probably shouldn't have. he didn't think it was funny. obviously. but I did. and I'm pretty sure God did. more than that I felt He was proud of me. because He knew then and He knows now that I am His. with all my imperfections and sins. with all that I lack. with everything I am and I am not. I still give it all to Him. He knows that no one can take His place in my life.

He comes first for me. always. what He says goes. with questions. and doubts. and tears. and lots of prayers. but it goes. I'll follow Him anywhere. and He knows that.

He knows that the changes He's made in me will not be undone by others. that's not to say I won't make mistakes. because I have. and we all do. I'm not perfect and I don't pretend to be.

but we do our best. and we hold on stubbornly to our God and to the changes He makes in us.

so when you come home, take your time. figure things out for y o u . accept the fall. don't wait for it. then pick yourself up again. the process is different for everyone.

but we all walk the same path.

I was a mess when I came home. I felt clunky and awkward. couldn't find a rhythm. there were so many different things that needed my time and attention. and they were all justified. school. work. church. friends. family. etc. there was so much going on and I didn't know what took priority. it was overwhelming.

so let me tell you what I learned.

it is 100% okay to feel whatever emotion you're experiencing in any given moment.

you can feel inadequate or uncomfortable. or happy and peaceful. you can yell and cry. or you can smile and relax. feel what you need to feel. you're feeling it for a reason.

coming home is a shift. and it's hard. everything is new but familiar at the same time. because you've changed. and now you get to decide which direction your life goes.

on the mission you were focused. you had a purpose. you served others all day long every single day. now coming home, your schedule is your own. your decisions and time are focused more on yourself than on other people.

it can be confusing. and numbing. and painful. and frustrating. and yet we're told "it's simple." to "pick up where we left off." to "adjust." and "to be normal again."

let's go back to that word. normal. one of my biggest pet peeves. and it annoys me so freaking much. literally on top of the list. probably number two next to people walking around with untied shoelaces. and honestly I don't know why that one gets me so much but it just does.

so, pet peeve number one ::

n o r m a l .

I hate that word. so, so much.

go look up the definition. and come back.

yeah I mean it. go.

the definition of normal is to c o n f o r m . to conform basically means to bend over and obey. to a standard that is usual. or typical. or expected.

so tell me. where in all the holy scriptures or current revelation from our prophets do we hear of our Savior, Jesus Christ, ever conforming? to anything? or to anyone besides God Himself? and where does it say that we are told to conform? to anyone? or to anything? besides God Himself?

it doesn't.

to conform is not in our nature. we are children of the God of the universe. all of us. I don't care what religion you practice or what deity you do or do no worship. we are children of Deity. our purpose is clear. we came here to follow our Savior, Jesus Christ. He was the perfect example.

the only standard Christ holds Himself to is the one set by God :: His gospel.
the gospel of Jesus Christ as taught by ancient and modern revelation through the church of Jesus Christ of Latter-day Saints.

and that should be our standard too. our only standard.

that's it.

and nothing more.

so for a returned missionary to come home after serving their Savior, Jesus Christ, and God Himself for an extended period of time and be told it's time to go back to being normal? to come back to the real world?

first, what is that even supposed to mean. and second, I can't really think of something more insulting to say to a returned missionary.

and I was insulted when it was said to me.

I remember feeling so frustrated. I had just spent eighteen months serving and following Christ. and it was life-changing. that sure felt like the real world to me. that sure felt normal to me.

it satisfied my soul more than anything else ever had.

I learned what it meant to be a disciple of Christ. and I never wanted to lose that feeling. that became my normal. and it continues to be my normal. because His is the only normal that matters. and His normal is discipleship. loyal, committed discipleship. any other definition of normal besides that doesn't come from God. it comes from satan. and we'll get to that later.

but this is a fight you'll have for the rest of your life. so take time to find out what your normal is. define it for yourself. because yours will be different than mine. all that matters is that it involves Christ. and that you're willing to let Him change it with you. He needs to be at the center of the life you're building.

so that's pet peeve number one. normal.

pet peeve number two ::

have you a d j u s t e d yet?

so annoying. most of the time, they were asking if I was adjusted to "normal life" yet and we all know how I feel about that.

so I'd always ask . . . am I adjusted to what? and they'd respond with oh you know, "being a normal person again" or "coming back to reality" or "getting back into a normal lifestyle" or "starting a real adult life."

and I would sigh. deeply. mentally throat punch them. and then tell them that I was happy and still figuring things out. because in my heart all I wanted to do was go back. and so by their definition, no. I was not adjusted. and I didn't want to be.

I didn't know what I wanted. but I knew what I didn't want. and I didn't want to settle. I didn't want to normalize or adjust. I knew what those words meant for them. and that's not what they meant for me.

why would God do that?

why would He teach us and change us just so we could come home and "adjust" and move on? throw it all away?

He wouldn't.

and we shouldn't either.

everything He taught us was meant to last. for the rest of our lives.

He taught us how to be disciples. and that did not end when we came home. what ended was the calling of being a missionary. actually being set apart by priesthood authority to act and teach and speak in the name of Jesus Christ. that ended. that authority is gone once you come home.

but the call to follow Him does not end. ever.

that's why we came to earth. to enjoy life. to learn. to grow. to succeed. to fail. to sin. to repent. to love. to hurt. to follow Christ. and understanding our purpose here on this earth can help us understand our purpose post-mission life.

because it's the same thing.
here's how I see it.

our souls miss living with God. miss being with Him. a lot.

He is God of the universe. He is the Father of our souls. and deep down we miss being with Him. miss that peace and happiness. that holiness.

and so we try to find Him. try to fill that void. we look for truth. and we follow it. we want to be close to God. and why wouldn't we? He is our Father after all. and serving a mission lets you feel that every. single. day.

the thing is, when we do find Him, we usually don't want to leave again.

take Alma for example. Alma was speaking to his son Helaman. telling him about his conversion story. Alma experienced awful pain. and then incredible joy. but what he says next is just beautiful. and sacred.

"methought I saw . . . God sitting upon his throne, surrounded with numberless concourses of angels, in the attitude of singing and praising their God;

y e a , a n d m y s o u l d i d l o n g t o b e t h e r e ."

Alma. one of the great prophets of his time. missed his heavenly home. missed being in the presence of His God. His Father. it's natural. our souls long to be home. long to be close to Him. always. and that's not wrong. it's such a deep part of who we are as e t e r n a l beings.

but what Alma does next is c r u c i a l . and it's something we have to choose to do too.

"but behold my limbs did receive their strength again, and

I s t o o d u p o n m y f e e t ,

and did manifest unto the people that I had been born of God" (*The Book of Mormon,* Alma 36: 22-23).

he chose to stand back up. to follow Christ. and to testify of God.

we chose to come here. we left our spiritual, heavenly home so that we could come to earth. get physical bodies. follow Christ. gain experience. and go back home. when we serve a mission, we sacrifice time and self to serve God. we feel that peace. and happiness. and holiness that comes from representing Him.

so naturally, we feel more distanced from Him after coming home. we feel longing. and loss. and grief. not because He is not there, but because we have to seek to find Him again. in a different way. He never left. our role in His kingdom just shifted. so when it gets hard. we grieve. and He grieves with us. and then at some point, we have to choose to stand up again and testify of Christ.

even when it's hard.

when I came home, I wasn't happy. or at peace. my joy was gone. and no one seemed to understand what I was feeling. and so I didn't open up about it. and the few times I did the advice I got was to let it go. to relax. to adjust to normal life. and that would eventually make me feel fine again.

but it did not rest with my soul.

I'm not saying the mission is the peak of this life. but it is one of them. it's a unique, sacred experience that shouldn't just be abandoned. or forgotten. so you have to decide what adjusted means to you. just like I had to decide what it meant for myself.

if adjusted meant I went back to being the same person I was before.
then no. I never adjusted.

if adjusted meant I stopped asking God to guide my life every day.
then no. I never adjusted.

if adjusted meant I put God in second place in my life.
then no. I never adjusted.

we
must
STOP

treating the mission like a phase or some neat experience.

any encounter with God is sacred. beautiful. and should be respected. acted upon. and lived. not forgotten. or watered down. or mocked. or abandoned.

watering down sacred experiences makes it i m p o s s i b l e to live the gospel the way it was meant to be lived. big. fully. whole. that's how it's meant to be lived. and the mission was one of those experiences meant to teach you how to live the gospel big. spiritual experiences are meant to last. they are meant to change us.

and how you choose to "adjust" when you come home will make the difference in your post-mission life.

because it is a h u g e mistake to think that God's expectations for us change after we come home from serving a mission.

that's the fall. the fall that you don't need to feel. it stems from the lie that God no longer needs you. that His expectations have changed. that it's okay to just move on and live some normal, adjusted life. and that sacred experiences are not as important as we make them out to be. that is the lie. and accepting that lie is how we fall.

that's when you need to decide what you will do. if you will master the fall. or fall apart.

coming home isn't a choice. falling isn't a choice. falling apart is though. think about our tree analogy again. you don't climb a tree expecting to let go of the branches and fall. nobody thinks like that. literally. so why do we think like that spiritually?

climb spiritual heights with God. and don't expect to fall apart afterwards.

expect to come back down. you have to. we all have to. but choose to do so gracefully instead of falling apart. you can. and He will be there with you the whole time.

we follow Him. we love Him. He is our Savior. He is our Brother. He is the Son of God. and He loves us. everything has more purpose and meaning and lasting power to it when He is here. present. in the day to day. that's exactly where He wants to be too. in the details. walking with us every single step of the way.

the day to day.

its hard. enduring to the end really sucks sometimes. living is hard. figuring out what to do with your life is confusing. I'm not going to lie. coming home is not easy. and if you think it is, you're kidding yourself, honestly.

nothing in this life was meant to come easy. but it is e a s i e r when He is with us. not doing everything for us. but walking with us. guiding us.

serving a mission teaches you how to follow Jesus Christ no matter what.

and if you did it right, it taught you that following Him is the only way to live this life. happily.

He is the only way. especially when things get hard.

I have a pretty intense fear of water. it takes a lot for me to actually get in the water. and it's rare that I swim. so my favorite part of swimming is coming up for air. naturally. breaking through the surface. feeling the pressure lift off my lungs. my mind can relax. I take in air. and light. and can breathe again. finally. deeply.

that's how trials are too. you've been holding your ground for so long. trusting that things will be okay. trying to stay afloat or just not take in water. and then it ends. you break through the surface. feel the pressure lift off your soul. your mind can relax. you take in air. and light. and hope. and you can breathe again. finally. deeply. you realize it's over. and done. because all hard times end. yes. all hard times end.

but until they end, you have to fight.

keep pushing through. keep holding your ground. keep praying for love. and light. and guidance. keep walking. no one is asking you to sprint. and God isn't expecting you to give any more than you can.

so just keep walking.

think about the pioneers almost 200 years ago. the ones who walked across the United States. on hope. and faith. walked. pulling their families and everything they owned with them. walking. through the heat. and the snow. day after day.

how did they do it?

first, they focused on who they were following. Christ.

and then they walked.

they put one foot in front of the other. and they walked.

that's it. literally.

you just need to walk.

and when you feel like you can't walk anymore, "hold fast to what you already know and stand strong until additional knowledge comes" as Elder Jeffrey R. Holland said (Holland, 2013).

that's what you do.

that's what I did when I came home and my world went dark.

I held still. I stood my ground. I prayed. I trusted God. I waited patiently. and not so patiently. and I watched. I did what I knew worked in the past. and I waited. until I surfaced again. until the hard times passed. until I could see again. and breathe again. and then I started walking again.

I learned to stop worrying about what I was doing wrong. and I started thanking God for staying by my side.

He is there. always. for me. and for you.

so don't be "normal." don't "adjust." don't "move on." don't go back to being the same person doing the same things you did before.

don't fall apart when it's hard.

and don't fall apart when it's easy.

the mission was meant to change you. permanently. change is good. and it's important to keep changing and to keep growing.

you will make mistakes.

God counted on it.

and He sent His Son Jesus Christ to sacrifice His life for us so that when we make those mistakes we can repent. we can change. we can pick ourselves back up and we can keep walking.

that name tag was removed from my chest. and yours was too. but my discipleship was not attached to it. and neither was yours. it could have been. and that would have been tragic. when discipleship is attached to the name tag, missionaries come home and leave it all behind. they feel the fall. and they fall apart.

following Christ is not something just missionaries do.

discipleship has to stay deep. like we learn in the Old Testament of the Bible, "I will . . . write it in their hearts; and will be their God, and they shall be my people" (*The Bible,* Jeremiah 31:33).

discipleship. following Christ. is supposed to be written in our hearts. so deeply connected to our souls that we understand that He is our God. and we are His people. forever.

my mom always told me that not a single day would go by for the rest of my life when I would not think about my mission.

and she was right.

I don't think I realized how much I would miss it. and I still do miss it. more than I can even stand some days. I miss everything about Uruguay. the rain. the people. the culture. the simplicity. the beauty. the goodness. the love. I miss being a missionary. serving Him every single day. serving His other children. seeing His word and His love change their hearts. and I miss being a part of that.

and I'm sure you miss it too.

so I'm going to level with you.

it's hard to replicate those deep feelings outside of full-time missionary service. it's not impossible. but the feeling that comes with representing Jesus Christ and teaching people about Him. that's something deep. and sacred. and unique to full-time missionary service.

I'm not saying we can't feel God's love and serve others after the mission. it's just different. that is one of the only callings on this earth that asks us to completely consecrate our lives to Him. and that was our calling. 24 / 7 .

so coming home and serving Him is going to feel different.

and it's okay to miss that.

God changed your heart. He woke your soul.

we did not come to this earth to be normal people who lived normal lives run by society and natural desires and lukewarm discipleship. so please don't forget why you're here. don't forget your purpose.

we are not part-time disciples.

we came here to follow Jesus Christ. if nothing else, that's what your mission taught you. and that's what you taught other people. so please. please do not forget that.

I remember one particular night after coming home. I was in the kitchen washing dishes. no one else was home. I looked out the window at the same view I'd grown up with for most of my life. I saw the same neighbors' houses. the same sunset. the same street. the same trees. the same cars. everything had stayed the same.

except for me.

I'd changed. so much. I felt out of place. and I was starting to fall apart.

I remember that moment. and I probably will forever. I asked God what I was supposed to do. I asked Him why it was so hard to follow Him. why I felt so alone. and out of place. why I couldn't find Him as easily as I had before.

and then that familiar, sweet spirit I'd come to know and trust so dearly entered the kitchen. and filled the room. and my heart warmed as I felt His arms around me.

and I realized I had a choice.

I could just let go right then and there.

I really could. I could forget about it all. I could leave the mission behind. in the past. I could go back to being the same girl who grew up on that same street with the same neighbors and the same sunsets and the same trees and the same memories.

and it would be easy.

pre-mission me was a good person. she was kind to people. she was friendly. she always went to church. she was good. and if I chose to be her again, I wouldn't have to try so hard anymore. I could stop fighting to follow Christ. I could stop feeling alone. and out of place. I could live a good, happy life. in my own little world. I could live within my limits. within my comfort zone. I could be a normal person. and live a normal life.

and then my soul began to ache . and I began to weep .

because God reminded me. I felt in my heart the sweetest, most gentle voice of His Spirit. reminding me that however familiar this place was to me. and however familiar this environment was to me.

it was not my home.

I was not from this place. and I could not go back to the life I led before.

because however good that girl was before, she was not a disciple of Christ. she hadn't learned that yet. and I knew in that sweet, sacred moment that if I let go. if I stopped following Christ. if I stopped giving Him my whole heart. I would regret it.

for the rest of my life. for eternity.

until I stood before God our Father on the judgment day and was held accountable to Him for the decisions I had made. or that I had not made.

because in that day it will not have been enough to just have been good.

I knew it. and God knew it.

and if you really sit down and look within your heart you'll know it too.

so I decided that night that yes. it was worth the fight. it was worth the discomfort. and the pain. and it would be worth anything else that ever came. to follow Him.

it is not enough to come home and just be good. I know that. and you know that. and God knows that. so be more. follow Him. strengthen your testimony. trust Him. do the best you can. and pray always. He will come.

let me say that again for the people in the back.

when you pray to God, your Father. H e w i l l c o m e .

you will feel His peace. and love. and strength.

His promise still stands :: "I will be on your right hand and on your left, and my Spirit shall be in your hearts, and mine angels round about you, to bear you up" (*The Doctrine and Covenants*. 84:88).

the Atonement of Jesus Christ lets the imperfect people (u s) be imperfect while becoming better. so don't give up. please don't. you've got this. and when you don't, He does.

you're going to make it. I promise. the sun will shine again. the clouds will clear. and you'll be okay. but you can't give up.

and don't let the nice, well-meaning people tell you how life is supposed to be after the mission.

don't let them tell you how to adjust. or that it is time to wake up and come back to the real world. don't let them tell you that your faithful service has ended. or that now it's your turn to live for yourself.

because you and I both know that's not how it's meant to be.

and more importantly, you and God know that's not how it's meant to be.

there are so many voices. everywhere. all the time. telling you where to go. and what to do. and who to become. they're logical. and believable. but there's only one voice that really matters.

it's not your mom's. it's not your dad's. or your bishop's. or stake president's. your institute teacher's. or best friend's. your neighbor's. your uncle's. or your grandpa's. or anyone else's for that matter.

the only voice that matters is God's.

but you already knew that.

our God is a just God. a God with a plan. who loves us. and does not want us to conform. He expects more. He Himself said "for behold, this is my work and my glory—to bring to pass the immortality and eternal life of man" (*The Pearl of Great Price,* Moses 1:39). that's His job. His role. His desire for us. to help us return home to His presence.

that's why His voice matters.

because His voice is the only voice consistently guiding us home. 24 / 7 . every single minute. of every single day. it is Him. speaking to us calmly. and kindly. gently. through His spirit.

asking us to follow His Son.

and He knows it'll be a sacrifice. and a lot of mini sacrifices.

but He'll be there the whole time. guiding us with His voice. the voice you need to come to know. and love. and crave. and trust. and listen to. especially when it's hard. the voice I hope you came to know before baptism. and on the mission. as Elder Jeffrey R. Holland said, "after an encounter with the living Son of the living God, nothing is ever again to be as it was before" (Holland, 2012).

the world changes daily. we change daily. and He changes us daily. and His voice is the only constant through any and all changes we'll ever go through. so learning to listen to H I S voice. and trust H I S voice. is crucial.

now don't misunderstand. He's going to speak to you through other people. through family. friends. church leaders. and others. you just have to learn to tell the difference. learn to pull the truth out of what is being said and follow it.

but listen for His voice everywhere.

because He knows. we're human. we get distracted. we get confused. and we forget to listen. let's be real. I know I forget to listen for His voice.

and then I hear it.

through a friend. or a family member. through a song. or a scripture. His gentle voice pulling at my soul. reminding me that I am His. and that He wants me to follow Him.

so I turn. and repent. and change. and follow Him again.

that's how life goes. and that's okay.

just follow His voice.

even if it contradicts the voice of a loved one. a family member. a friend. or your own thoughts.

He will lead us down paths we do not know. and ask us to trust Him. He will call us alone. and ask us to sacrifice. and to follow Him.

and it is our choice to go or to stay.

but happiness and safety will come from following His voice. n o m a t t e r w h a t .

learn to trust Him. and listen to Him. and follow Him. fearlessly. President Russell M. Nelson said that "in coming days, it will not be possible to survive spiritually without the guiding, directing, comforting, and constant influence of the Holy Ghost" (Nelson, 2018).

come to know His voice. it is so important that you do.

learn to receive personal revelation. answers from God about your life for yourself. those answers are for you. and you alone. and what I'm learning is that honestly, they might not make much sense to others. and that's okay.

you do not have to convince a n y o n e of the reality of what God has asked you to do.

personal revelation. you and God. not you and me and God. not you and your parents and God. just you and God. through the power of the Holy Ghost.

because you need your Savior. I need my Savior.

we need Him.

and He lets us choose whether or not we want to listen.

but He will always speak to us plainly. so that we understand. and if the answer isn't plain and simple, then we're asking the wrong questions. the prophet Nephi says "for he speaketh unto men according to . . . their understanding" (*The Book of Mormon,* 2 Nephi 31:3).

God always wants us to understand His will for us. why wouldn't He? we just need to ask. and then listen for the answer.

normal people make normal decisions by themselves that affect the course of their normal lives.

but that is not us.

we are eternal beings who make eternal decisions with God's help that affect the course of our eternal lives.

and Christ came first. to set the example for us.

He said, "behold I have given unto you my gospel . . . that I came into the world to do the will of my Father, because my Father sent me" (*The Book of Mormon,* 3 Nephi 27:13).

Christ came to do the will of His Father. and so did we. that's what experiences like serving a mission teach us.

it's not easy being home. it's not easy knowing I can never go back to that part of my life. I think at least for me, that's where the pain stems from.

but as John stated, "we love him, because he first loved us" (*The Bible*, 1 John 4:19). we only know pain because we first knew love. and the loyalty and love we need to follow Him comes from knowing how much He loves us. whether we follow Him or not.

He changed me on the mission. stripped away all of the expectations and the drama and the doubts. and reminded me that I am His daughter. and that I am here to follow His Son.

I want you to feel the same thing. if you haven't already. and I want you to understand that it's your choice.

our discipleship did not begin when we were baptized. or when we were set apart as full-time missionaries. it began in the premortal life when we all chose to follow Christ down here to earth.

that was the beginning.

the mission is just one of those sacred experiences that reminds us of why we're here. and teaches us how to be disciples in this world.

but our discipleship did not begin here. and it won't end here either.

it ends when we are called home to the presence of our God. and maybe not even then.

so you can't just set aside some time for God every now and then and expect to be happy. and fulfilled. you can't go back to your normal life and hope He is there and present.

He has to be at the center of our lives.

always.
and that shouldn't change just because you came home.

watching that airplane descend into my home state. stepping off that plane into a familiar environment. picking up a familiar routine. literally nothing around me had changed.

but I had.

and I knew that I would never be the same.

how much trust does that show from our Father in Heaven that He would take us out of our homes. teach us. shape us. mold us into dedicated disciples. and then send us back into the exact same environment we came from.

and trust that we wouldn't go back to being the same people?

so much trust.

and love.

you were not meant to go back to being the same person. the mission was not just a neat experience. you were supposed to change. and to hold those changes sacred. and to change the world around you.

He came back home with you. you walked for Him there. and He walks with you now.

so keep Him close. follow His ways. continue to change. and grow. and be His disciple.

that is why we're here, after all.

3 ::

ok. we're going to get real again.

about satan.

because behind every doubt. and fear. and confusing time. is one common denominator.

satan.

and you need to get to know him. I know that sounds weird. but it's true. and important. because he is real. and evil. and wants more than anything else to destroy us.

so yeah. I'm writing a chapter about him. so that you know how to recognize his influence in your life. especially in your post-mission life. and how to deal with it.

so let's circle back to our tree analogy again. when you believe that you're going to fall apart. when you give up hope that you'll reach those spiritual heights again. when you choose not to master the fall. when you choose to leave the path of discipleship.

you open the door for satan.

he is our enemy. our adversary. and while we don't need to fear him, we also shouldn't underestimate him.

he is incapable of doing good.

he cannot be reasoned with.
he cannot be tolerated.
he cannot be listened to.

and he has to be shut down. daily.

I remember very clearly a line from a priesthood blessing I received not long after I came home from the mission ::

satan toys with your depression like a puppet on a string.

and that's when I realized he is not just unkind or mean. he is not just a son of God who chose the wrong path.

no.

he is the very definition of evil. he is the father of all lies. he is the creator of havoc. and pain. and destruction. he doesn't just want to get in our way. or trip us up. or cause pain and contention. he doesn't just want to hurt us.

he hates us.

and his goals are greater than to merely inconvenience us.

he wants to destroy us.

completely.

in every way possible.

mentally. emotionally. physically. spiritually.

he wants us to forget who we are. why we are here. what we learned on the mission. he wants to break you. to pieces. to tear you from the side of your Heavenly Father. to strip you of hope. and peace. and comfort. he wants to make sure you never make it back home to God's presence.

he is the leader of the damned. the exact opposite of God. there is no light or goodness or hope about him or for him.

God created the world. and satan is trying to destroy it.
God created you. and satan is trying to destroy you.

because you chose to follow Christ and come to this earth. you chose Christ instead of him. and he hates you. he hates you for being baptized. for having spiritual experiences. and for being able to grow closer to a beautiful, eternal life that he can never have.

he hates you for serving a mission. for helping others come to know Christ. and you need to understand that as a missionary, you were protected from satan on a deeper level than you are now. because your role was different.

now you're home. and that calling you had to represent Christ directly every single day has ended. and so that deeper level of protection has ended. so now you're satan's new target.

so trust me. and believe me. when I tell you just how important it is that you come to know and recognize and trust the voice of your Father in Heaven. the voice of Christ. your Savior.

it is c r u c i a l to your spiritual survival.

it's also important for you to recognize the voice of satan.

let me explain.

we were each given the light of Christ. the innate ability to know the difference between truth and error. a conscience in other words. and that comes from God. you have that. I have that. everyone on this earth has that. because they are a child of God and it's a gift from Him.

so take that one step further. and put in place a divine filter.

we know that "no man can serve two masters" (*The Bible,* Matthew 6:24). that we need to "choose ye this day whom ye will serve" (*The Bible,* Joshua 24:15). and that "my sheep hear my voice, and I know them, and they follow me" (*The Bible,* John 10:27). these are all truths we know. promises we know.

so start applying them.

because let's be real here. technically you aren't really listening to anyone when you don't know whose voice you follow. and if you aren't listening to God, you're listening to satan. it's simple.

so one of your post-mission challenges is to learn to determine who and where your thoughts come from. i n s t a n t l y .

so learn to implement a d i v i n e f i l t e r .

because everything you hear, read, see, learn, experience comes from God or from satan.

yes. everything.

now I'm not a black and white person. at all. I see a world of colors. and possibilities. and it's hard for me to only see black and white like some people can.

but. when it comes to the thoughts that enter our minds, that is black and white for me.

every time.

your thoughts should pass through these gates ::

is this God speaking to me? or is this satan?

that's it. I'm serious. this will make S U C H a difference for you.

because you know the voice of God. God is light. goodness. clarity. simplicity. hope. kindness. charity. His voice sounds like I'm sure it would if he were standing here in front of us. speaking with us.

the voice of satan though is always changing. lies. confusion. contradictions. doubts. questions light and goodness. mocks. creates darkness. selfishness. and frustration.

he is the opposite of our God.

so it makes sense that his voice would be the opposite too.

but that matters less.

what matters is your relationship with God. that you learn to speak with Him. and recognize His voice. it matters that you know that He loves you. and that you look to Him for help. regularly.

it matters.

I really don't like the question "are these thoughts from God or are they my thoughts?"

because by asking it, we're overcomplicating one of the simplest things ::

communicating with God.

if it's good, it's from God. if it's not good, it's from satan.

simple.

and we have to learn to recognize the difference. because we're at war.

and no, I'm not being dramatic.

you and I and everyone else here who has lived and will ever live was born in the middle of a war. between God and satan. right and wrong. good and evil.

think about the great council in heaven before this life began. we chose to follow Jesus Christ. or to follow satan. one third of our brothers and sisters chose to follow satan. and they never came to earth. the other two thirds chose to follow Jesus Christ. and they are here. every single person ever born or ever to be born on this earth chose to follow Jesus Christ. how deeply committed they were, I don't know. but I know they're here now.

and they chose Christ at one point in their life. remember that. when life gets hard.

you chose Christ once. you beat satan once. and the fact that you're standing here today is proof.

so you can beat him again.

our spirits are at war. and our thoughts are always being influenced. by God. or by satan.

so simplify it.

you know what is right and what is wrong. what is good and what is not.

what is good comes from God and what is not comes from satan. so it's up to you to learn to recognize the voice of your God. instead of doubting Him.

I call it a divine filter.

ask yourself. if God were standing in front of you right now, would He be saying to you these things you're thinking? and there's your answer.

it's that simple.

I'm sure that of all the trials God knew we would go through in this life, one of the saddest for Him to know was that there would be times when we would not hear His voice. He is our Father. and He loves us. and wants us to hear Him. always.
it's worth the time and the effort to come to know His voice. using a divine filter brings hope. and clarity. it calms the confusion. and it helps you distinguish His voice from satan's.

when you recognize your thoughts are from satan, just get rid of them.

s e n d   t h e m   b a c k   t o   h e l l

there'll be truth in what he says. he's clever like that. but there's one truth you must understand ::

God does not use satan to speak to His children .

e v e r

God doesn't speak in partial truths. He doesn't shame us. or embarrass us. or speak to us negatively. He will not use darkness or evil to speak to His children.

He will correct us. gently. remind us of our purpose. of His Son's Atonement. He will touch our hearts and invite us to repent. with love. and firmness. but always with love.

that is the voice of our God. of our Father. and He loves us.

satan does not love us.

he doesn't even like us.

he actually hates us.

and I don't like him either. to be honest.

he is literally the worst. nothing good comes from him because there is nothing good about him. and he doesn't want to help us.

so knowing all that, why would you ever want to listen to or take advice from someone like that?

he's got nothing of value to say. so he's not worth listening to. it's that simple.

what he says will have truth to it. almost always. he speaks to our doubts. and insecurities. our questions. and desire for validation. he tells us partial truths.

but partial truths are lies.

so don't listen to him. use that divine filter and ignore literally everything he says.

he could be 100% right about what he's saying. about that weakness you have. about those doubts you have. but it doesn't matter. because God does not use satan to speak to His children.

whatever needs to be addressed, He will tell you Himself. in a kinder, more loving way. with your best interests at heart. through His Holy Spirit. the third member of the Godhead. and that's it. so even if there's truth to what satan is telling you, it still does not come from God. because God does not use satan to speak to His children. and He never will.

so whatever satan's telling you, let it go.

one of my mission companions taught me a hugely important lesson I'll never forget. it was about taking advice from people. people you know, people you don't know. church leaders or family. strangers or friends. whoever it might be. don't take advice from everyone. yes, God speaks to us through other people, but He will do so in His way.

so what someone tells you out of hatred. ignore it. out of jealousy. ignore it. in a painful or negative way. ignore it. doesn't matter if it's true. if it comes to you in a negative way, ignore it. because if it really is truly necessary and you need correction or change.

He will send someone else to tell you. someone kinder and more loving to correct you with

l o v e and c o m p a s s i o n .

He teaches with love. not shame. and with respect. not disrespect.

so ignore them. and wait for Him to teach you.

because He will.

I mentioned it a little earlier, but I want to talk about it again.

guilt.

we all know what it feels like. it sucks. and it's one of satan's tools.

please remember that guilt does not come from God.

I repeat... guilt does not come from God.

remorse. yes. guilt. no.

God will never tell you you're not good enough for Him. He will never tell you to live in fear. or to constantly watch your back. to worry all the time. to feel ashamed of your mistakes to the point that you feel you can't move forward. He won't tell you to live a perfect life. and it's not Him that causes you to feel shame when you make a mistake.

that is not our God. that is not His voice.

our God speaks with love. firm love. He corrects us when we're wrong. warns us when we risk making poor choices for our lives. invites us to repent. we feel remorse that leads to a desire to change. not guilt that shames us.

so stop listening to satan. stop paying him any attention at all. it's just not worth it.

another one of satan's tools :: guilt for temptations.

you and I and all of us need to stop repenting for temptations. if you haven't sinned, you don't need to repent. so stop. his temptations are not your sins. the pain he causes is not your responsibility. stop feeling guilt for being tempted and having a hard time.

rely on the Atonement of our Savior, Jesus Christ. He loves us. He cares about us. He makes all of our wrongs right again. when we repent. and change. He lets us choose. and then sanctifies those choices. makes them holy. or He helps us correct them.

remember how much He truly deeply loves you.

and then remember.

r e m e m b e r :: i t w a s s a t a n

i t w a s s a t a n . who wanted to give us O N E single chance to return to the presence of God. who wanted to force us all to think the same. act the same. make the same decisions. be the same person. live the same life.

i t w a s s a t a n . who wanted to strip us of our individuality. and by so doing, strip us of our right to choose anything. and everything.

i t w a s s a t a n . who wanted us to believe we are all the same and that God expects us all to be the same.

look at the difference.

people are different. the gospel is the same.

people are different. the gospel is the same.

p e o p l e a r e d i f f e r e n t . t h e g o s p e l i s t h e s a m e .

God does not expect you or me to b e p e r f e c t .
He wants to help us b e c o m e p e r f e c t .

His Son. our Brother. Jesus Christ. atoned for our sins and sacrificed His life for us. so that I can be me. and so that you can be you. so that I can find God. so that you can find God. and so that we can all repent. change. and start over. again. and again. and again.

we are not meant to fit a mold. we are meant to follow a Savior.

there is no o n e single way to live the gospel of Jesus Christ. we live by the gospel and teachings He set forth. but most importantly. we follow Christ.

think about that third of our brothers and sisters. the ones who chose to follow satan. sometimes I wonder if they left not because they lacked faith in Christ and in His ability to save them. but because they lacked faith in themselves and their ability to follow Him.

I can't guarantee that's why some of them left . . . its not doctrine. just an idea. but I catch myself feeling that way sometimes. and that comes from satan. when we don't feel worthy enough to follow Christ. holy enough. strong enough. knowledgeable enough. overall good enough. and the guilt just climbs until we just decide not to follow Him.

that comes from satan.

satan tells us we're not enough to follow Christ. not God. satan tells us the Atonement of Christ can't help us. because we're not good enough. because of our past. our mistakes. our doubts. our questions. our weaknesses. he tries to make us feel like we have to meet some standard before we can follow Christ. before we can pray to God. before we can repent and change and become better. or start over.

that's from satan. not God. and it's a lie.

it's a very logical lie. it makes too much sense. hurts more than we want to admit.

but it's still a lie.

when satan can't attack our faith in Christ, he attacks our faith in ourselves. and our faith in our ability to follow Christ.

he bullies us. shames us. discourages us.

and it frustrates me.

who is he to tell any one of us that we are not capable of following Christ when he never even tried to? he could have. and he chose not to. and his mistake is not ours.

every. single. time. we take a step closer to God, two things happen ::

God blesses us.

and satan attacks us.

coming home from the mission brings with it a certain vulnerability. similar to the vulnerability that comes after being baptized. or repenting. or making any covenant with God, really. when we recommit ourselves to Him. or we sacrifice for Him. or we try to come closer to Him. we make ourselves vulnerable to God.

and satan attacks. tells us we aren't ready to follow God. or that our past disqualifies us. he attacks our weaknesses. our insecurities. our flaws. our fears. and he guilts us. shames us. sends those thoughts that tell us we're not good enough. not holy enough. not knowledgeable enough.

and that's simply not true.

we are always good enough for God.

I am always good enough for God.

you are always good enough for God.

good enough. holy enough. knowledgeable enough. and no mistake you make or doubt you have or fear that comes takes that away from you. you cannot lose His love. you cannot lose His support. it's not even an option.

our God does not have qualifiers for receiving His love. He asks that we follow His Son. not because He won't love us if we don't. but so that we can a l w a y s feel His love. so that we are never alone. so that we can find relief from the burdens we carry. so that we can hear His voice. and so that the power of the Atonement of His Son Jesus Christ can wipe away the guilt. and the shame. and the fear. that He did not ever want us to feel.

so.
breathe.
relax.
listen to the voice of your Savior.

y o u   a r e   e n o u g h   f o r   G o d .   y o u r   F a t h e r .

so then what other voice even matters?

none. the answer is none. His voice. His calming. gentle. voice. is the o n l y voice that matters.

I don't write in my journal often. okay. I actually never write in my journal. at all. so this experience was distinct for me to actually feel the need to write about it. it happened about ten months after I got home.

November 20, 2015 — 2:28 a.m. . . .

fear limits progress. we know that. and I feel limited right now. like I'm regressing. I'm going backwards when I should be going forward. and it's frustrating. makes me angry. makes me feel bitter towards others and mostly towards myself.

but it's a conscious decision we need to make. right? to let go of fear and hold to faith. it doesn't just happen that faith miraculously wins over and all fear is instantly gone. no. if I want this fear to go away, I need to actively and passionately fight against it. but today it's too hard.

he's screaming at me again. mentally. emotionally. the satan who chases me is loud. cruel. unforgiving. relentless. he. never. stops. and he screams at me. tells me I'm worthless. I'm a failure. that I've let God down. that I'm not enough because I'm not a missionary anymore. and I think I believe him sometimes.

all he does is scream guilt and shame at me. every. single. day. and I've been letting him. some of the things he says are true. all his screaming and fighting and anger is getting to me. the regret and anger at myself for coming home. for not being a perfect student. daughter. sister. friend. coworker. for not being a perfect disciple. for not knowing all the answers to gospel questions. for missing promptings. or for being too tired to follow them sometimes.

I don't feel like I'm enough. sometimes he screams at me so loudly I can't hear the Spirit whisper at all.

but then I do. I hear Him calming me. quietly. gently. reminding me that satan hates me. hates us all. but that he always fights the hardest when we're walking towards God. when we're trying. he fights the hardest just before we turn to the Savior. just before He comes to us.

. . .

he still screams at me the same way today. sometimes I recognize it in time. other times, it takes me a while to realize what's going on and to shut him out again.

it helps me to picture what God would say. if He were standing here. in front of me. He wouldn't tell me I'm not enough. He would tell me to turn to His Son for help. for peace.

God is our Father. He love us. wants us to be happy. without being worried about making mistakes. we have scars. and that's okay. Christ does too. our scars show us where we've been and the sacrifices we've made. so do His.

His scars hold the power to heal our wounds. to heal our souls. and comfort our hearts. to dry our eyes. to quiet our minds. and to bring us peace. to help us grow stronger. or to just hold us when we can't go on.

we've all heard it before but I want to mention it again. nobody criticizes a baby for falling over when she's learning to walk. nobody judges her. she's learning something new. she could stop. but there's a part of her soul. instinct. that knows she is born to do more than sit. or crawl. so she stands. and falls. and stands again. and falls again. until she learns to walk. and then she still falls at times. for the rest of her life. she is not immune to falling just because she learns to walk. but her soul knows she is meant to walk. so she gets up and she walks over and over and over again.

you are not meant to sit. or crawl.

your soul knows that. it's instinctual.

so stand up. and walk. follow Christ. and fall. and then get back up. and follow Him again. for a thousand different steps. in a thousand different ways. you will follow Him. and you will fall. and you will repent. and you will stand up. and follow Him. and fall again. over and over and over again. for the rest of your life.

because you are not meant to sit. or crawl.

because you are not meant to to feel ashamed. or to doubt. or to fear.

and your soul knows that.

it is a deep, innate part of who you are to follow Him. so don't stop.

faith only takes us forward. fear only takes us backwards. so if you're going backwards. stop. that's not faith. that's not from God. and you need to cut it off. so just stop.

stop thinking that way. stop acting that way. stop doubting yourself. stop criticizing yourself. stop punishing yourself for things that Christ can heal for you. stop doubting.

and look to Christ.

love Him.
trust Him.
follow Him.

and stop doubting your ability to follow Him.

that's another one of satan's tools :: doubts.

doubts do not come from God. ever. period. He specifically tells us "look unto me in every thought; doubt not, fear not" (*The Doctrine and Covenants.* 6:36). doubts don't come from God. they'll run you around in circles. depress you. confuse you. and ultimately lead you to resent God. to turn away from Him.

don't confuse questions with doubts.

questions come from a place of confidence and curiosity. they help us search for understanding. they look for reasons to learn. to believe. to gather information. to make educated decisions.

doubts come from a place of uncertainty and fear. they stop our search for understanding. they look for reasons to disprove. to fear. to ridicule. to abandon or back away from forward progress.

it's okay to have questions about the gospel. to have there be things you don't understand. things that don't make sense. it's okay to question those things and find answers. that's healthy. that's how testimonies grow. by questioning. and by learning.

it's not healthy to doubt the gospel. to find reasons to disprove it. to fear and to ridicule the things that aren't easily understood. to back away from God or Christ or His gospel because it requires commitment.

a doubt is just a question you don't want to put in the effort to find the answer to.

that's how satan breaks us. by turning healthy questions into unhealthy doubts. by telling us it's too confusing. or it doesn't make sense. or it shouldn't be this hard to follow God.

umm okay. listen.

FOLLOWING CHRIST IS SIMPLE. NOT EASY.

do you know who said it was simple? God.

do you know who said it was easy? satan.

Alma told his son Helaman "do not let us be slothful because of the *easiness of the way*; for so was it with our fathers; for so it was prepared for them, that if they would look they might live; even so it is with us . . . yea, see that ye look to God and live" (*The Book of Mormon*, Alma 37:46-47).

the easiness of the way. not the easiness of what was asked of them or of us. not the easiness of life. not the easiness of trials. not the easiness of building testimony. not the easiness of following Christ. just the easiness of the way. it is simple to follow Christ. but it is not easy.

Elder Jeffrey R. Holland put it more beautifully than I ever could ::

how could we believe it would be easy for us when it was never, ever easy for Him?

I'm not talking about anything anywhere near what Christ experienced . . . but I believe that . . . to come to the truth, to come to salvation, to know something of this price that has been paid, [we] will have to pay a token of that same price.

for that reason I don't believe missionary work has ever been easy, nor that conversion is, nor that retention is, nor that continued faithfulness is. I believe it is supposed to require some effort, something from the depths of our soul . . .

if you wonder if there isn't an easier way, you should remember you are not the first one to ask that. someone a lot greater and a lot grander asked a long time ago if there wasn't an easier way.

when you struggle . . . you are standing with the best life this world has ever known, the only pure and perfect life ever lived. you have reason to stand tall and be grateful that the Living Son of the Living God knows all about your sorrows and afflictions.

the only way to salvation is through Gethsemane and on to Calvary. the only way to eternity is through Him. the Way, the Truth, and the Life (Holland, 2000).

do you see it? do you feel it? this is bigger than you and me. this is deeper than our doubts. this is a decision we need to make every single day to follow Jesus Christ. not because it is easy. but because it's the only way back home. it's the only way our families can be together forever.

H E is the only way.

so when doubts come, which they will. identify them. figure out what satan is trying to cover up or make unclear. turn them into questions. and then ask God to help you find the answers.

let your questions guide you to God. chasing your doubts is a long, difficult journey that takes you away from Him. away from peace and answers. it creates confusion. and chaos. and breaks down trust with God.

another one of satan's tools :: isolation

satan wants us to feel alone. isolated. like we're the only ones suffering. or struggling. or having a hard time. wants us to feel like no one understands us. like we have to suffer alone. he twists the example our Savior left us. tells us that Christ was alone in His trials, and so we too must be alone in our trials. satan tells us that seeking out help will somehow invalidate our trials.

that. is. such. a. lie.

it's. just. not. true.

Christ had His Father. He was not alone. and He lived a perfect life.

W H Y ?

so that we would never. e v e r . E V E R . have to walk alone.

that doesn't guarantee that this life will be easy. and it doesn't guarantee that we won't at one point or another have to choose between following others or following

God. and sometimes that will require walking alone. physically. but never, ever spiritually.

see isolation and walking alone aren't the same thing. one is a tool of satan. the other is a requirement of God.

think about it.

Moses in the wilderness.
Joseph of Egypt in prison.
Job and all he suffered.
Daniel in the lions' den.
David and Goliath.
Noah and the ark.
Jesus Christ in Gethsemane.
Nephi and Sam leaving their brothers.
Alma and the wicked king Noah.
Joseph Smith in liberty jail.

and many many more of God's followers have had to walk alone. even for a brief period of time. they had to leave their families. their homes. they had to sacrifice comfort. and familiarity. health. some had to sacrifice everything.

they walked alone. to follow their God. and satan tried to isolate them. but God stayed with them.

they were able to tell the difference. if not at first, then later. they learned as must we, that God does not isolate His children from Him. there will be times when He will ask us to walk alone. to sacrifice. and to leave all to follow Him.

but God does not isolate His children.

He does not leave us.
He does not forget us.
He does not abandon us.

He will always. always be there for His children.

knowing that, we can walk alone with God. and be okay with it. there will be times when we are called to walk alone. to leave family. friends. comforts. to walk alone to follow God. to choose Him over the alternative.

but even in those moments. you are not alone.

kneel down. pray. then stop. and listen.

f i n d H i m .

and He will come.

following Christ does not isolate us. it separates us. yes. but it does not isolate us. it does not make us feel lonely and separate. or unworthy of love and companionship. like isolation does. and if that's what following Christ makes you feel. then pause. reassess. and find your why again.

because even when we follow Christ alone. we don't need to be lonely.

so when He calls you to go. go. I love the scripture that reads "how beautiful upon the mountains are the feet of him that bringeth good tidings" (*The Bible*, Isaiah 52:7).

the f e e t . of all the things Isaiah could have talked about, he talked about feet. not about minds. not faces. not hands. not the hearts. he chose the f e e t .

why?

because feet follow. feet don't question. they aren't there to impress. feet don't draw the attention to themselves. feet walk. they follow the mind that guides them up the mountain. feet put into action the will and intent of the mind guiding them.

they don't argue. they don't complain. they just walk. one step after another.

we walked in my mission. every area. every companion. every. single. day. we walked. in one of my areas it took forty-five minutes just to get to the halfway mark. forty-five minutes. of nothing but walking. speed walking mind you. forty-five minutes. every single day.

and I remember being so tired. and in pain. but my feet. my feet never gave out. we called them our automatic legs because no matter how tired we were they never quit. we would come home many nights and patch up blisters. blisters we didn't realize we'd been walking on all day. we were tired. our feet were tired. they were sore. but when our minds said walk. our feet walked.

I wore through at least three pairs of shoes on my mission. but my feet never gave in. and I was more grateful for them than for anything else.

think about the Last Supper.

Christ's last night with His disciples.

He didn't wash their heads. or their hands. or their clothing. or their faces.

He washed their feet. their dirty feet.

He washed those feet that had followed Him tirelessly for the past three years. the feet that had just listened. had just obeyed. had just followed Him. without question.

one of the last things our Savior. the Son of God. did during his life on earth was wash feet.

and it's a beautiful lesson.

He feels our pain. and He values our obedience.
He heals our pain. and He values our discipleship.

possibly more than anything else.

become the disciple to Him that your feet are to you. if He calls you to go. go. satan tries so hard to get us to stop. to give up. to lose hope. to question our steps. to stop following our Savior.

it's a choice.

a choice to continue to follow Christ. and a choice to ignore satan. he is our enemy. as we mentioned before. and every day he causes us to slip up. or to fall. in small ways. and in large ways. satan has that ability to bring us down.

but that ability is countered by the Atonement of Jesus Christ. the healing power our Savior possesses to lift us up. to heal us. to mend the slip ups. and the falls. the small ones. and the large ones too.

falling is a part of life. making mistakes is a part of life. it can't be avoided. it was never meant to be avoided. but it can be repaired. it can be healed.

w e   c a n   b e   h e a l e d .

no matter what we've done or where we've been. no fall is too great. no mistake too deep. no error too damaging.

Jesus Christ is our Savior.

and He can save us. and heal us. He wants to heal us. always. He makes our fall mean something. we don't need to wait for the fall when we know He is right there to help us through it all.

so satan can tempt. and beat down. and hurt. and belittle. all. day. long. and he will.

but the moment you turn your heart to the Savior. the moment you reach out in prayer. the moment your knees hit the ground and you call upon His name. it's over. satan has lost his power. and you're free. again. and again. and again. safe in the arms of your Savior.

we don't run out of chances with Christ. ever. I mean seriously. n e v e r .

y o u c a n n o t f a l l b e y o n d C h r i s t ' s a b i l i t y t o s a v e y o u .

I promise you that. if there is one thing I know about our Savior, it is that truth. His love saves. His grace is enough. for all of us. individually. over. and over again.

satan never quits. never stops. never gets bored. he changes his tactics and his angles daily. and while we might forget who we are at times. we have to realize he remembers us. he knows you. and he knows me. he was once our brother. he learned with us. grew with us. knows our potential. what the veil in this life requires that we learn by faith, he already knows.

so use it to your advantage.

when he presses the hardest. does his worst to destroy. or to make afraid. pause. pray. and find out what he's trying so hard to cover up. what truth he's trying to bury. what answer from God he's trying to misinterpret.

I am grateful to satan for one thing. and one thing alone. that he tries so hard to destroy me. because in doing so, he pushes me even closer to my Savior. because when he tries to tear my world apart, I run to the One who heals. the One who protects. the One who saves. and I know that in His arms I am safe.

and the same is true for you. always.

satan wouldn't care if you weren't trying to follow Christ. and his opposition and anger reminds us that this is a war. between good and evil. and we need to choose. every single day whose side we're on.

we need to fight to follow our Savior.

when it's easy. and when it's hard. we all go through ups and downs in life. some days are harder than others. way harder. so on the days when you can't move forward. don't.

just stop.

and stand still.

and let God stand with you.

when you don't know what to do. or where to turn. or who to listen to. stop. breathe. and find Christ. hold to your truths. trust your Savior. and know that things will get better.

remember who you are following. remember why. and let Him hold you. and comfort you. support you. and love you.

trials will always come. from God to make us stronger. from our own decisions. from the decisions of others. from living a human, mortal life. but God is always on our side. satan is the one who makes trials miserable. not God. and we choose what we will learn from them.

trials either build us up. or break us down. that's what we always hear. let's be real. they do both. trials build us up and break us down. every single time.

falling down is not a failure. but choosing not to get back up is.

we all have our demons. our weaknesses. our trials. our addictions. illnesses. disorders. of the physical, mental, emotional, or spiritual kind. we all struggle. no one is exempt from that.

it's similar to the story of the sons of Helaman in the Book of Mormon.

after fighting one of their hardest battles, he says "there was not one soul of them who did perish; yea, and neither was there one soul among them who had not received many wounds" (*The Book of Mormon,* Alma 57:25).

you will see so many beautiful times in this life. so many joyful, glorious times. but you will also see so many hard times. so many difficulties. we all will.

and just like the sons of Helaman. we can come out alive. exhausted. weakened. wounded. but alive. and stronger. knowing better the God in whom we trust.

so get to know your demons. your sins. your weaknesses. your tendencies. don't be ashamed of them. be humble and willing to take them to God and deal with them. and fix them. one at a time.

it starts with honesty. being honest with yourself first. so you can go to Christ with an open mind and heart. so you can find healing. and grow.

turn to Him and become whole again. or find comfort until you can be made whole again.

and trust that you are not alone.

satan likes to isolate us. tell us we're alone. that we have to fight our demons and our battles alone. he tells us we're the only ones struggling with xyz. and that we should be ashamed.

and that's just not true.

because of your identity as a child of God, you are never alone.

I'll say it a g a i n .

b e c a u s e w e a r e c h i l d r e n o f G o d , w e a r e n e v e r a l o n e .

whether we follow Him or not. whether we believe in Him or not.

God is still our F a t h e r .

Christ is still our B r o t h e r .

we are still children of D e i t y .

the fight between good and evil in the world is not over. and the fight between right and wrong within each of us is not over.

it is satan who tells us that we have fought the good fight. that we have done our part by serving a mission. that our discipleship has ended. and that now it's our turn to rest.

dear brothers and sisters. we have not fought the good fight. we have only begun to fight it. we have not done our part after serving a mission. our discipleship never ends. and it is not our turn to rest until God Himself spreads His arms and welcomes us into His presence again.

we follow the voice of Jesus Christ. our Savior. until we're called home. satan doesn't have a say in the work of the Lord. and it's not over just because he decides to speak up.

dismiss satan. daily. because he literally has n o t h i n g to say worth listening to.

you are a child of God. please don't forget it.

4 ::

so let's recap. you fell out of the tree. you're home. you've stood up. and brushed yourself off. you've decided to continue to follow Christ. you've implemented a divine filter. and you actively dismiss satan every day.

you're doing your best to follow Christ. to find a rhythm. and belonging.

so now what?

coming home from a mission is overwhelming. there are so many emotions, feelings, decisions, paths to take, etc.

the world is open to you.

and it's exciting.

let me give you a few tips and pointers.

f i r s t :: don't let your missionary service be the best time of your life. I don't want you to be eighty years old looking back and still telling everyone the mission was the best time of your life and nothing will ever compare.

no.

the mission was

o n e of the best times of your life.
o n e of your most sacred experiences.
o n e of the most life-changing times you've ever experienced.

but it can't be the only one.

missionary service in your early twenties is not the peak of mortal life. it can be one of the peaks.

God wants us to be happy. remember? to have joy and to follow Christ. He wants you to live a beautiful, full life. a happy life. filled with amazing experiences and memories. He wants you to climb lots of trees. and fall out of lots of trees. not just the mission.

the mission taught you how to live the gospel. so remember it. refer back to it. love it. live it. learn from it. and carry it with you.

go live. be happy. love God. and make beautiful memories. live your life with as much passion and joy as you possibly can. and follow Christ with your whole heart. take what you learned and live it. don't forget it. teach it. live it. pass it on. and trust that is how God meant for it to be.

its okay to miss your mission. I've been home five years. and I still miss it. so, so much. more on that in the next chapter though.

s e c o n d :: part of your call to serve God was to love the people with whom you served. and to love the people you met. and taught.

that call did not end when your name tag was removed.

stay in contact with those sweet people you came to love. your companions. other missionaries. kind people you met and loved. people who you taught and helped to baptize. people whose testimonies you strengthened.

we were all brothers and sisters before we came to earth. before we went to different families. and cities. different countries. and races. different nationalities. and cultures. and religions.

we were brothers and sisters. and we still are.

I don't believe in coincidence. not even a little.

the people you met. that was for a reason. the people you crossed paths with. for a reason. the people you served with. for a reason. your companions. your mission president. all of that was intentional.

so live intentionally.

if you can stay in touch with those people. then do it. talk to them. be their friend. strengthen them. keep testifying of Christ. keep following Him. and keep encouraging them to follow Him.

your mission ended. your discipleship didn't. when Christ finished His mission. He went back. He went back to visit the people He loved and taught. He went back. He loved them. He prayed with them. He strengthened them.

and we should do our best to follow His example.

in their eyes, you will always be that young missionary. the one who stopped them in the street to talk to them. the one who reminded them what it felt like to feel God's love. the one who showed them who God was. the one who taught them of Jesus Christ. their Savior. their Brother.

you were the instrument God used to love His children. to teach them. to be there for them. to help them feel His love. to help them want to follow His Son. to help them come closer to Him than maybe they ever had before.

your mission changed you. but it most certainly changed them as well. and you can't just walk away from that.

don't forget about them. don't leave them out of your life. God let you change their lives. just as He let them change yours. He crossed your paths for a reason and I doubt it was just to say hello.

those relationships were meant to last. eternally.

t h i r d :: you will make mistakes.

some will be small. and minor. others will be large. and lasting. there have been times when the Spirit was not able to stand with me. or when I chose to distance myself from God. there have been times when I sinned. accidentally. other times it was on purpose.

and if there is one lesson I am learning more than any other, it is just how deep God's love is for us. and just how deep the Atonement of Jesus Christ can extend for us. Their love is deep. Their forgiveness is deep. Christ's power to save is deep. so much deeper than we will ever realize and than we will ever be able to overuse.

I do not say these things to justify sinning. or to encourage a casual attitude towards making mistakes. I do not say these things to make it seem like the Atonement of Jesus Christ is something to be taken lightly or misused.

I say these things because I want you to know. I need you to know. that your sins and your mistakes do not define you. they do not disqualify you from God's love. and they do not need to stand in the way of you becoming whole again.

God loves you. so much that He sent His Son Jesus Christ to come to earth. to suffer for your sins and your mistakes. to die. and to resurrect. for one reason.

so that you and I would have a Savior.

Jesus Christ is our Savior.

He saves us from our sins. from our mistakes. saves us from the influence of satan. saves us from ourselves. from our imperfections. from our one-time sins. and from our continuous sins. He saves us from anything and everything that could ever possibly stand in the way of our coming home to live with God again.

His love is deep. deeper than we could ever understand. or exhaust.

you cannot sin beyond His ability to save you. so long as you are willing to repent. and give all to follow him and become whole again.

to become whole is a process. over and over and over. it's not a one-time event.

to sin after coming home from the mission is not a failure. it happens. it's as much a part of this mortal life as is our ability to be forgiven.

and what we choose to do after we have sinned will always be more important than whatever sin we committed or whatever mistake we made.

we can start over.
we can be forgiven.
we can be saved.

what is required of us is that we follow Christ.

think of discipleship as a tree.

trees start from seeds. weak. fragile seeds. they need water. soil. air. and time. and then they can start to grow.

there's no rush. they take their time. and grow tall. they go through storms and push roots deep into the ground. they bear fruit. they give shade. and home. and coverage. they bring color to the world. and beauty. they give life. and air.

they can be cut back. but it only makes them grow taller. and straighter.

think about it.

trees don't need anything from us. they need sunlight. air. water. and time. all they need is God.

discipleship starts as a seed. a small, fragile desire to believe. small steps. constant learning. and time. lots of time. there's no rush.

discipleship is a lifetime journey. not a set of steps. it takes time. we learn. and then grow. we go through hard times and push roots deep into the ground. sometimes we are cut back. only so that we grow stronger. more sure. determined.

it's simple. not easy. but simple.

be stubborn in your discipleship. be stubborn in following Christ. when you make mistakes, repent. change. and go again.

to repent is to change. that's literally it. nothing huge. or unachievable. repentance is change. and it's us deciding to follow Christ again.

God does not want perfection. He wants loyalty. He wants us to stay. He doesn't want us to run away in shame when we sin. or distance ourselves when we make mistakes.

He wants us here. in front of Him. in all our mess.

He wants to know that we will turn to His Son over. and over. and over again. every time we struggle. every time we make mistakes. every time we want to give up.

He wants us to stay. no matter what happens. no matter what we do.

He wants us to stay. and to follow Christ.

in the best way we know how. because there's no one specific way to follow Christ.

remember :: people are different. the gospel is the same.

you have specific gifts. and talents. strengths. perspectives. that are different from others. that are special. and unique. and from God.

so go figure out what they are. turn them into strengths. and then use them to make a difference. use them to testify of Christ. to follow Him.

I struggled with feelings of uselessness when I came home. in the mission, I knew I was making a difference. I was working hard. I was a leader. and an example. I knew what I was doing. and I felt needed.

then I came home and felt lost. left out. confused. and useless. very useless.

and I'm sure I'm not the only one who has ever felt this way.

remember what we talked about earlier. your calling to serve as a full-time missionary has ended. but your role as a disciple has not.

you are still needed.
you are still loved.
you are still wanted.

it's just different now.

think about it like this.

how many tools does it take to build a house?

can you do it all with a hammer? no. what about a screwdriver? nope. a staple gun? also no.

you need so many tools to build a house. you need a hammer. nails. screwdriver. table saw. measuring tape. wrenches. the list is huge. I've only named the most basic, obvious ones too. you need all sorts of tools that do all sorts of different things to build the same house.

you can't build the kingdom of God with just a hammer.

or a whole army of hammers.

no.

you need all sorts of tools that do all sorts of different things to build the same kingdom.

serving a mission teaches you a few ways to build the kingdom of God. go out and teach. baptize. spread the word of God to everyone you meet. hammer roles if you will.

you were that hammer. you served in that specific role for an extended period of time. and now that you're home, that's not your job anymore.

you can still pick up a hammer from time to time if you want. but it's not your calling twenty-four hours a day, seven days a week like it was before.

it is S O important that you find out what God needs you to do here. that you find out who He sees that you can become. your talents matter. your likes and dislikes matter. your strengths and weaknesses matter. all of that will guide you to become the best version of yourself so that you can feel full and complete and useful in God's kingdom.

there is no one way to build a house. and it most definitely isn't done with just one tool.

it was never part of His plan for us to all be the same. to have the same goals. to live the same life. to do the same things. to feel the same way about everything.

we are different. we have different goals. perspectives. talents. strengths. mindsets.

God knows that. and He respects that. He meant for it to be that way.

and He loves us. so much. He wants us to be happy. and to be ourselves.

so if you're not a hammer, don't be a hammer. don't stress yourself out. if you're not comfortable doing xyz to spread the gospel then don't do it. find what works for you. find out who God can help you become. and then go do it.

for example. I typically don't like to bring up church talk in conversations. especially if it's not already the topic. it feels forced and unnatural to me most of the time. so I usually don't do it. but I love answering questions. I'm not an expert. and I don't have all the answers. but if someone has questions about what I believe, I'm ready and happy to do my best to share.

that is the tool I'm comfortable with. the tool that aligns with me. so I use it. and I don't try to force something I'm not comfortable with. if the Spirit prompts me to use another tool, then I do my best. but I'm not going to stress about it. it should be natural. and comfortable.

that is why I love ministering. so much. because it follows this same mindset we've been talking about. it's an invitation to go love and serve and help people.

in the way that y o u know how.
in the way that is comfortable for y o u .
and most importantly, in the way that is comfortable for t h e m .

the people you minister to. they should feel loved. and respected. you're building a friendship. no script. no expectations. no standards. there's no one way to minister. it's just loving people. in the way you know how and in the way they need.

God needs you to be yourself. the purest, strongest version of yourself. so that you can enjoy this life. and follow Christ in the way y o u know how. and bring joy to others. so that you can tell others of Him.

when you are living as y o u and following H i m . they will find H i m through y o u .

your discipleship hasn't ended. it's just shifted. take the time to grow closer to God in different ways. and notice how you will still see His hand in your life. notice how you will see yourself fit into His kingdom more fully. more deeply.

I love Alma's question :: "if ye have experienced a change of heart . . . can ye feel so now?" (*The Book of Mormon,* Alma 5:26).

I remember coming home from the mission and stressing out because I worried I wasn't feeling the Spirit as strongly. worrying that I was doing it all wrong. worrying about everything and nothing at the same time. but this scripture always comforted me. because I could still feel that change of heart. I could feel His love. I could still feel the changes that He had made within me.

and that's true for all of us. in all of our sacred experiences.

the change of heart from baptism. or from your answered prayer. from temple covenants. or missionary service. from any sacred experience that touched you. changed you.

you have the right to feel those changes again. those are your sacred experiences. they changed you. and the reason he asks if we can feel that change of heart or not is because it's possible to feel it again. and again. and again.

especially with His help.

I know He's helped me. countless times.

when you come home, you go from one role to many. from a missionary to a disciple. student. employee. child. adult. sibling. friend. leader. etc.

it was simpler on the mission.

you were a missionary. and that was it.

it takes time to figure things out when you come home. and that's okay. but holding onto those changes of heart you had can help.

take your time to figure out your next steps. and if you get asked what they are, remember.

first :: you don't have to answer.

not everyone who asks you has a right to know. and it's okay to say you're not sure. even if you are sure. your business is your own.

second :: respect your process.

don't be ashamed if you're working a minimum wage job. or still trying to find work. don't be ashamed if you're just starting college. or if you have no idea what you want to do with your life.

if you have a plan. or if you don't.

you are enough. you're doing just fine. and you have time. so much time.

just follow christ.

that's why we're here. and when that decision to follow Him guides our lives, everything takes on more purpose and meaning.

Christ doesn't want perfection. He wants loyalty.

we are imperfect people following a perfect Savior. and He knows that. and loves us still.

so go be imperfect and follow Him. talk of Him. live for Him. and others will see it. and their hearts will stir. and they too will find Him.

there will be days when it will be harder to find Him. I don't know why. some days are just harder. some days are easier. I think that's just life. and life is all about growing and learning. making mistakes and trying again. it's about

living happily and following Christ.

so on those days when it's hard to follow Him or to even find Him. relax. it doesn't mean you did anything wrong. sometimes it doesn't mean anything at all.

just go find Him. and talk to Him.

He is there.

I promise.

our God is our Father. of all of us. always. when we follow Him and when we don't. our God is a God who loves His children. our God is a God who stands with us. always.

if you feel you can't find Him. pray. He is there.

do the things you've done before to feel His love. pray. go to the temple. go to church. read the Book of Mormon. or the Bible. or conference talks. pray. ask for a priesthood blessing. walk through nature.

I love the verse "ask, and it shall be given you; seek, and ye shall find; knock, and it shall be opened unto you" (*The Bible*, Luke 11:9).

that's a promise. from God. that when we look for Him. we will find Him. that when we need Him. He will be there for us.

that is our God.

He knows us. and we know Him.

I remember the first day of my mission. we were all sitting there listening to our new mission president speak. he was talking about prayer and receiving answers. at one point he started knocking on the table. he asked us what he was doing.

knocking. we said.

he continued to knock and asked us what he was doing. we were worried we had misunderstood. so nobody answered.

and then he quoted that scripture I just mentioned above.

"knock, and it shall be opened unto you" (*The Bible*, Luke 11:9).

and then keep knocking. he said. and keep knocking after that.

too often we stop after the first knock. we stop after the first answer we receive. and then we wonder why God doesn't speak to us more.

knock more. and then listen. he said. keep knocking until further revelation comes. and until you understand His will on a deeper level.

so knock. and if you don't get an answer. keep knocking. knock until the answers come. pray until you feel Him answer your prayers. if the answers aren't coming. keep knocking.

He is there. He is listening. and He loves you.

even when you don't believe it.

one of my sweet companions taught me an important lesson about finding Christ.

I was about two months into the mission. and I was frustrated. so frustrated with myself. my spanish wasn't great. I couldn't understand people. I knew I had so much to learn about the gospel. and it wasn't coming fast enough. I wasn't learning fast enough. and I felt lonely. and very inadequate. I didn't feel like I shouldn't represent the Lord because I felt like I didn't know anything. like I wasn't enough.

in very broken spanish, I explained all this to my companion. she said nothing. instead she took me to the bathroom. stood me in front of a mirror. and told me to look.

look. she said.

look until you see Him there. in you. until you see your divinity. until you see your spiritual DNA that links you to Him.

and she made me stand there in front of the mirror looking at myself.

I was uncomfortable. obviously. and after about five seconds, I tried to leave the bathroom. but she stopped me.

she said I don't care how long it takes. or how uncomfortable you get. two minutes. ten minutes. thirty minutes. you stand there. she said. and look into your eyes until you see Him. until you remember who you are. until you remember that you are His child. and you feel it again.

and then she walked out and shut the bathroom door behind her.

so I stood there. looking at myself. I'm not sure how long it took before I saw Him. before I saw that divinity within myself. before I remembered that I was His child. a child of God. before I felt His love and His peace fill my heart.

and it changed me. it really did.

I still stand in front of the mirror from time to time. and just look.

we are human. we make mistakes. we struggle. we are not perfect. and we have a lot to learn. but none of that changes the fact that we are children of God. of a God who loves us. who wants us to succeed. a God who wants us to know that we are His and that He will never. ever leave us.

so.

when you can't find Christ.
when your purpose is unclear.
when you feel lost.

when you feel like you are not good enough for Him.

go stand in front of the mirror and look.

look until you see Him in you. look until you see your divinity again. look until you remember who you are. and you see your soul light up. look until you feel His love burn within you again.

look until you find Him. He's with you. always.

as a missionary, you wore His name on a tag on your chest. you testified of Him. you represented Him. people saw you and came to know God through the Spirit that you carried to them.

and then you came home. and that name tag was removed from your chest.

but you should still feel it. feel that desire to follow Him. feel His love. feel your worth. and know that no matter what happens, your worth never changes.

He loves us deeply. we are His children. and He is always with us.

I love one particular story about Alma. at one point he just got so frustrated. so frustrated with where he was at and with his limitations. he wanted to be more. to do more. more than what he had been called to do. he wanted God to use him. to build him into something greater.

he said "O that I were an angel, and could have the wish of mine heart, that I might go forth and speak with the trump of God, with a voice to shake the earth, and cry repentance unto every people" (*The Book of Mormon,* Alma 29:1).

and he goes on to talk about how he longs to feel that way again. how he longs to be more. and do more.

maybe you've felt that way before too. I know I have.

on your mission. after your mission. after your baptism. or some other time. that ache to do more. to be more. to know your full potential. and to live it. that aching soul comes because we are His. and while our capacity is mortal. our potential is eternal. so we begin to feel this discontent.

it's an itch that can't be scratched. an ache that can't be soothed. a feeling that can't be ignored.

when your soul aches to follow your Savior. and to be His.

so when that ache comes, turn to him. because He can do what we cannot. He knows all. sees all. guides all. and He loves you. and me. in His hands we can become more whole. more complete.

let that ache grow within you and push you. push you to Him. let it touch your heart and change you. change your mindset. when your soul aches. turn to God.

He needs you. in all your untapped power. and potential. He needs you. in all your weakness. and frailty. and insecurities. because pebbles make waves too. and He needs you.

He made you the way you are for a reason. so find your reason. and live it. for the rest of your life. come home and fight along. follow those achings. let them guide your growth.

follow Christ. it's not easy. but it is simple. and that is where we will find our joy. in Him.

be strong. He loves you. you are stronger than you think. and He knows your potential. so when He tells you to dig deeper. dig deeper. when He pushes you to the limits of your faith. be strong. be brave. be bold. be happy. speak out. stand up for what is right. and defend it. kindly.

watch Him make you stronger and more capable than you ever thought you could be. with the faith and power you give Him.

to be timid is not in your nature. you are a child of God.

"doubt not; fear not" (*Doctrine and Covenants.* 6:36). over. and over. and over again.

be strong. hold on to hope. hope is never. ever. lost. and you are enough for Him. always.

on a side note. right after I came home, one of my institute teachers asked me for a list of the most important things returned missionaries should know. he asked me what things I was doing to help in those moments when I didn't know what to do or how I was supposed to feel. so here's a go-to list. if you're stuck. or in a rut. or need an idea of how to get moving again.

1. stay in contact with people in your mission. they need you and you need them.
2. write to the missionaries in your mission you knew and left behind.
3. spend time. don't waste time on social media. it can be a great tool for missionary work.
4. study the scriptures. *The Holy Bible. The Book of Mormon. The Doctrine & Covenants.*
5. attend the temple regularly.
6. pray deeper than you do right now.
7. take the Sacrament.
8. work in the temple if possible.
9. keep planning. your week. your month. your future.
10. read *Preach My Gospel.* and apply it.
11. serve someone. every single day.
12. keep listening to good music. not exclusively. but don't cut it out of your life.
13. go to God first.
14. study the words of the prophets regularly.
15. ask for a calling in your ward.
16. be friendly. say hello to people.
17. write to your mission president.
18. take time to nurture your soul. every day.
19. Alma 37:37—take it 100% literally. let Him guide you from your first step off that plane.
20. forgive yourself every night. and ask forgiveness. every night.
21. never go to bed angry.
22. trust the word of your church leaders. go to them for counsel and advice and comfort.
23. ask for advice from loved ones and leaders and peers. be teachable.
24. get priesthood blessings often.
25. feel whatever you're feeling and let it be valid. accept it. and ask the Lord to comfort you.
26. find something to laugh about. every day.
27. stay close to the Lord. your first loyalty is to Him. always.
28. just keep walking. some days you run. others you crawl. but don't ever stop progressing.
29. and take time to heal when you need it.

5 ::

so let's get real about feelings.

because coming home is hard.

and there's a lot of feelings involved.

whether you consider yourself to be an emotional person or not.

coming home from the mission is a huge life adjustment. and there is a lot to process. showing emotion is not weakness. and having a hard time does not reflect weakness. it doesn't reflect a lack of commitment. or an inability to cope. or whatever else you think it might reflect.

whatever you're feeling is justified. and you need to take time to heal.

I miss everything about the mission. I miss the good days. the bad days. the crying. the prayers. the soul ache we talked about. and for the longest time I wanted to go back.

let's be honest. sometimes I still do want to go back.

and that's 100% okay.

but I've hard to learn that I can't go back. and I can't "move on" either.

I hate that phrase.

"it's time to move on . . . moving on is the hardest part . . . have you moved on yet?"

ugh.

you can't just "move on" from a sacred experience that changed your life. that impacted you so deeply. you can't just bury something like that in the past.

it doesn't work that way.

you can't go back and live it again. but you also can't just let it go and forget about it either.

it's deeper than that.

Uruguay has my heart. and always will.

that's not going to change.

but I also don't live in the past every day and wish I could be there more than I am here today.

you aren't supposed to move on and forget about the mission. I didn't want to. so I never did. and now I'm here to tell you that you don't have to move on either.

your challenge is to move f o r w a r d .

see the difference?

let me explain.

to move on from something is to leave behind or abandon something. in the pursuit of something new. like a breakup. you move on. leave it in the past. find someone new. or an old job. you move on. you find a new job.

to move forward though is to take it with you. let it grow with you. let it guide you. like the skill set you learned from that old job. leave the job. take the skills you learned with you. or like your baptism. you don't just move on from that. you take it with you. you look back on it and think about it. you let it guide you.

when we leave our spiritual experiences behind us, we leave behind us our ability to change and to grow. we leave behind the patterns of change we learned. we leave behind us the way the Lord spoke to us and taught us.

and that's just not how it's supposed to work.

I love the concept of continuous change. it's something the mission teaches. change requires that things be different. different companions teach you different skills and mindsets. different areas teach you different teaching methods and different lessons. if something wasn't working, you changed it. if you weren't learning a concept one way, you changed your methods to learn it a different way.

the mission taught you to be flexible. moldable. humble. understanding. and willing to compromise and accept change.

so knowing that, I can guarantee that God did not intend for you to come home and get all set in your ways.

or to think that continuous change was a thing of your past.

doesn't even make any sense.

you know a lot. but you don't know everything. none of us do.

but knowing how to change. that's golden. and it is crucial to learning and progressing.

we all know how much I hated coming home from the mission. it was so hard for me.

God let me go through hell and back. ok let's be honest. I definitely made it harder on myself than it probably needed to be because I was unwilling to accept the change He had just given me.

I remember talking to my mission president a few months before I came home.

he said to me "sister, your time is coming to a close here. are you ready to go home?"

I told him no.

he laughed kindly and told me it would be okay.

but I turned to him and said "no. it won't. I'm serious. I don't want to go home. I need you to find a way for me to stay here."

and his eyes filled with tears. and so did mine. he told me he understood. and I saw in his eyes the same ache I knew he could see in mine. he felt my heartache.

and a few months later, I still had to come home.

and when I did, I felt it all. I experienced it all. I'm not even kidding. it was so, so hard. but God knew. and it needed to be that way so that I could write this book and help others.

I don't pretend to know everything. but I do know how hard coming home is. and I know what has helped me. I just want to help you and others get through this. I miss my missionary service. and that's okay.

and if you miss yours. that's okay too.

on the opposite side, I've known so many returned missionaries who say it's just too hard to be home and think about their missions. that it just hurts. it's too painful. so it's just easier to let it go and not think about it.

to those dear brothers and sisters. if that's how you're feeling. just pause. know that it's okay to feel that way. and that it's okay to hurt. it's okay to think about your mission. and cry. and miss it. it's okay to want to go back.

you're grieving too.

and our Savior grieves with you.

to grieve over a sacred experience is not a shameful thing. it is sacred. and special. and holy.

there was Another. much greater than you or me. who also grieved. because of the pain He felt. even though He knew everything would be okay. He still grieved. and He called upon the powers of heaven. and He was comforted.

we too can call upon the powers of heaven when we grieve. and we too can be comforted.

this is not our home. and I think we forget that sometimes. this life will be beautiful and difficult and everything in between. and then it'll end. and we'll go home. home to our Father in Heaven.

don't you think our spirits cry out at times? just wishing they could go back to their home?

I'm sure of it.

I've felt it.

that soul ache that pushes us to find God. that reminds us that we are His children. passing through this life to live it and love and become the best version of ourselves that we can.

that comes from God. and it's okay to feel that.

it's okay to miss your mission. just like it's okay to miss your heavenly home. would we ever want to go back home if we never missed it in the first place?

pain can bring about beautiful things. no, I did not say pain is a beautiful thing. because it's not. but it can bring about beautiful things.

think of a mother giving birth to her child. so much pain. and then love. overwhelming love.

see pain doesn't just generate out of nowhere. you have to do something first in order to experience pain. it's a "cause and effect" concept. in this case, pain is the result of another strong emotion :: love. deep love can bring about deep pain.

I can guarantee you miss the mission because you loved being there. and our souls miss our heavenly home because we miss being there.

pain causes a deeper appreciation. a deeper understanding. it forces growth.

the mission was one of those experiences when you got to experience all of that. and learn.

I'll bet you didn't know you could love a stranger so deeply. I'll bet you didn't realize just how much you were willing to sacrifice to help someone else find God. I'll bet you had no idea how happy you could be while hardly even thinking about yourself.

the mission taught you deep love. and deep pain.

you learned strength. and determination. to fight. and to push through opposition. and pain.

because you had no other choice.

you learned that God is your Father. and your Ally.

you learned that Jesus Christ is your Savior. He saves you. and me. from ourselves. and from anything that could ever possibly hurt us.

and He saves us out of love.

you learned deep love. because you felt deep love.

from God. and from Christ.

and that love hasn't changed and will not change just because you came home.

it hurts coming home. because that deep love is different. you're doing different thing at home than you were on the mission. you have different responsibilities. and goals. and daily tasks.

but that deep love is still there.

you're just going to feel it differently.

I gave it all to God on the mission. I'm not saying I always did the right thing. or that I was perfect. but I left it all on the table. gave every single part of me to Him. and asked Him to change me. to make me His.

and that is why coming home broke me.

because I felt that deep love. and it changed me.

and then I had to leave it all and come home.

I remember being so angry at God when I came home. it wasn't all the time. but there were moments. strong moments when I cried out. so angry that He could take away from me the most beautiful, life-changing experience I'd ever lived to that point.

I wanted to know. if He wanted me to be happy, then why did He break my heart. why did He let me fall so hard out of that stupid tree.

deep love.

that was the answer. the only answer I got.

every. single. time.

I was so annoyed for the first while. until I began to understand.

if God took away such a beautiful, holy experience. if He sent me home from a life-changing eighteen months. if He took away from me the thing that mattered the most to me. and let me fall. and break apart.

it was because He had something greater coming.

so much greater.

and He and His deep love knew and understood what I couldn't comprehend :: that what was coming was greater. and that I needed to trust Him.

I needed to fall. so that He could catch me. and wrap me up in His arms. and guide me on to greater things.

and that was hard to hear.

I was in so much pain when I came home. but that deep love got me through. helped me feel safe. and strong. and able to stand up and keep on walking. because I knew the God I trusted. and I knew that if He broke my heart He could put it back together.

and He did.

and I am so much stronger because of it.

deep love comes with deep pain. but it heals. and you grow back different. stronger.

going back to that first day of my mission. sitting there listening to my president talk about his mission. he had also served in Uruguay thirty-something years before. and he talked about how much he missed those people. how much the mission changed him. and how blessed he felt to be back in Uruguay again. serving.

and I saw it in his eyes. the nineteen-year-old missionary who had left his home so many years before to serve God. the missionary who gave God his whole heart and watched Him change it in front of his eyes. the missionary who grew into a man and felt God's deep love change him. that deep love that sank into his soul and changed his very nature.

I saw that on my first day in Uruguay. and my soul ached to feel it.

and then I saw the tears begin to fall. and run down his face.

and he let them fall. he didn't wipe them away. he didn't act embarrassed. didn't apologize for crying. didn't make excuses. nothing.

he let them fall.

that was the first day I really remember learning about deep love.

because I saw it in his eyes. and in the way he let his tears fall.

I learned that it's okay to feel pain. and sorrow. to grieve. it's okay to feel whatever emotion you're feeling. that is not weakness.

and especially coming home from the mission. deep love brings deep pain. and deep emotions.

and deep growth comes from respecting those deep emotions.

your mission was unique to you. and your experience coming home will be equally unique. I can't cover every scenario or emotion you'll feel coming home. I can't help you know how to deal with all of it. but I know how it was for me. and now you know how it is for you.

and Christ knows how it is for both of us. and His Atonement is a gift for both of us. for all of us.

healing comes from Him. always.

I don't have to see His face to know that He is my Savior. my Brother. my Friend. and neither do you. I don't have to know all the details of His life to know that He loves me. and neither do you. yet He does know the details of our lives. every messy, imperfect detail. and He loves us still.

there's no way He would have suffered and died for us if He didn't love us. and if He didn't want to help us grow. and heal. and go back home. He knows our pain. our deep pain. He felt it. and He loves us. deeply.

so trust Him. deeply.

with everything you have. all your faith. and strength. and love. all your fears. and imperfections. and weaknesses.

trust Him enough to give it all away. and then just live. and follow Him. and be happy.

don't lose hope. don't give up. don't forget who you are.

God loves you and will never leave you. Christ loves you and will always heal you.

trust them. deeply.

and watch yourself grow. deeply.

I was in a dark place when I came home from my mission. I didn't feel whole. I felt numb. I didn't feel a sense of accomplishment. I felt weak. and then at one point, I just stopped feeling at all. I couldn't think straight. I didn't enjoy things. anything. and the simplest thing became so hard. too hard. getting out of bed deserved a medal. not going back to bed after class or work was impossible. there was a dark void in my mind. constantly. and I felt like I was spinning out. like I was losing control.

and one of my dear institute teachers saw it. and stepped in. he convinced me to go be evaluated by a professional. so I did. and I was diagnosed with high-functioning clinical depression and a generalized anxiety disorder.

I was told there was a chemical imbalance in my brain that had been affecting me since childhood. I was started on medications and sent to counseling. and I went. but inside I rejected the diagnoses.

and I refused to accept the fact that I was broken.

I couldn't do it. it just seemed so weak to me.

it's not like I was dealing with anything new. I'd dealt with these feelings before the mission. during my teenage years. even back into childhood. and I had made it this far. so I wouldn't accept it. I'd learned to fight off the darkness. to work through the numbness. and the pain. my struggles weren't new to me. so why did they need a label now?

it was such a draining process.

but God knew what I would not accept.

and He was always there.

He placed enough stubborn people in my life to help me accept the fact that I needed help. from a stubborn institute teacher and encouraging grandparents. to a thorough doctor and a persistent therapist.

they all did their part to make me feel loved. and safe. not alone. and not responsible for what had happened.

I was suffering from a major depressive episode. it wasn't the first. and it wouldn't be the last.

but I was still in denial.

I told myself that returned missionaries didn't do this. I'd served God every single day. I was so strong for so long. and I did so many hard things. I told myself I couldn't come home and break. or fall apart.

I had just spent eighteen months helping other people find hope and find Christ. if I fell apart now I would be such a hypocrite. and God would be disappointed. if I accepted this diagnosis, I would be failing Him.

at least that's what I told myself.

here's what I learned.

Christ can't heal us until we accept that we need healing.

isn't that just the gentlest slap across the face? it was for me.

I remember sitting on the couch in the basement one night. everyone else was in bed and I was trying to do homework. and I just couldn't. I couldn't focus. I felt so extremely overwhelmed. and then I started to weep. hard.

so I knelt down and started to pray for help. I continued to weep as I felt myself approach that all-too-familiar void in my mind. that dark space. the cliff where if I fell again, it would take days or weeks to fight my way out of it again. I knew that darkness. the depression. and I knew it would be uncontrollable. and so, so difficult. I'd just spent weeks clawing my way out of that mental hellhole. and I wasn't ready to go back.

and then I felt His arms wrap around me.

and for one moment. all was still.

in that moment I saw what my Savior knew about me.

He knew how hard it was. every single day. how hard it was to just get up out of bed and live. how hard it was to do the simplest things.

He knew how much I missed the mission. and how hard it was to make peace with being home. He knew how hard it was for me to come to Him when I struggled. and He knew how sometimes I just couldn't do it.

so He came to me.

and He put His arms around me. and just held me. He knew I couldn't stop myself from falling again. so He intervened. and He caught me. and held me.

that night was a turning point for my soul and my mind and my health. I accepted the fact that I needed healing. that I needed my Savior. and by accepting that, I let Him in. and He came.

I admitted to myself that I was broken. for the first time since being home. but it was okay. because my Savior had come. and He had come to stay. He loved me even though I was broken.

I'm not going to lie and say it all got better. that my depression went away and I was whole again. that episode did end. and then another came. and that one ended. and later another came. and five years later, I'm still dealing with it. it might never go away. but neither will my Savior. and when the depression sets in, we fight it together.

whatever your post-mission experience might be. you need to find that safety in Christ. that deep love. understanding your relationship with Him, or developing a relationship with Him, brings peace and comfort and security.

we come to know our true potential when we realize how much we need Him in our lives. I need Him. every day. in every part of my life. I need Him. and sometimes I forget it. and then things fall apart. and then I turn. and He is there. He is my Savior. and I owe Him everything.

and all He wants is my loyalty. and all He wants from you is your loyalty. Christ asks us to follow Him. He has walked where we will walk. He has felt what we will feel. He is here. and He loves us still.

so when it gets hard. turn to Him. when you feel your weaknesses are just too intense. turn to Him. when you don't know which way to turn or what to expect. turn to Him. and follow Him.

He will come.

I'm not going to tell you to rejoice in your trials. I'm not that way. I don't like trials. ever. I complain. and question. and doubt. and get frustrated. and cry. a lot.

and that's okay. because that doesn't mean I'm failing.

and if you're that way too, it doesn't mean you're failing either.

because even when I'm doing all of that, my heart still wants to follow the Savior. and He knows that. and that's enough for Him.

He doesn't expect perfection. just loyalty.

you don't have to rejoice in your trials. but you should come to respect them.

respect the times that break you. knowing that they will build you stronger. respect the hard times when you wander around in darkness. knowing that you will love and appreciate the light once more. respect the times when you feel distanced from God. knowing that once you find Him again, you'll fight even harder to be with Him.

I don't rejoice for the hard times I went through. but I respect them.

they broke me. so that Christ could heal me.

He knows the nights you kneel down and cry out in pain. and sadness. and frustration. because He remembers the night when He knelt down and prayed for you. He remembers the night when He saw all of your sins and mistakes and everything you and I and all of us would and could ever do. and He decided to love us anyway. and decided to give His life for us anyway.

so that we could be saved.

that is love. deep love. deeper than you or I will ever fully understand. and it is given freely. the only thing He asks of us is that we follow Him. so that He can save us.

He remembers you. He knows you for who you are. and He loves you.

you are worthy of love. and respect. and forgiveness. follow Him. and find it.

even when we've sinned. maybe especially when we've sinned. His deep love reaches out. and heals. when we're not ready to repent. or maybe don't know how to. His deep love is still there.

you are not alone.

you can walk through those church doors every single sunday as an imperfect and loved child of God. and hold your head up. you can kneel and pray and still feel His love. you can still read from the holy scriptures and learn of Him. and of His will for you.

we cannot be saved without having sinned.

that's not an invitation to sin. but an acceptance. and a respect. Jesus Christ did not die to save perfect people. that was never the point of all of this. of any of this.

go live. happily. follow Christ. do the best you can.

and trust the path He leads you down. it will not be perfect. you will sin. and make mistakes. and that's okay. I can't stress that enough.

have the faith to be imperfect. trust that Christ's love is deep enough to save. because it is.

you are not lost to Him. and you are not a lost cause. ever. you are a child of God. and His love never changes. we are expected to grow from our mistakes.

which means we need to make them first.

so don't abandon your discipleship just because you cannot fully participate right now. it matters so much less to God what you can't do than what you are actually standing up and doing. so you can't go to the temple. then go to church. so you can't take the Sacrament. then pray and think of Him. so you can't stand and bear testimony. then bear it in your heart.

do what you can to repent and change. and when you're ready, go get help from church leaders.

but do not forsake your God. because He has not forsaken you.

your sins and your mistakes are not enough to drive Him away from you. so don't let them drive you away from Him.

you are not lost to Him.

keep following Christ. especially when it's hard. I promise it will get better. and it will get easier. the hard times are just a promise that better days are coming.

I love rain. so, so much. and it rains a ton in Uruguay. a ton.

and the only way to tell that the rain is coming is by what comes first :: the heat. the heat would come for a day or two or sometimes three. humid. sticky. blistering. nearly unbearable. heat. and then the clouds would gather. and break. and the rain would fall. finally. the sweet, fresh rain. would fall and cool everything down. cleanse and refresh everything. including us. almost to the point where we would forget how intense the heat had been.

our relief comes a f t e r our hardest trials.

after the pain and the discomfort. after we have suffered. and struggled. and fought for longer than we thought was possible. after we've sinned more than we think is forgivable. after we've been through everything we can handle. after we've seemed to reach our breaking point.

the rain will come.

and we will find relief.

so take hope.

and follow Christ.

when God is silent. when you can't hear His voice. when you can't feel His arms around you. when you wonder why He has left you.

don't lose hope. He is coming.

He is coming.

so hold on. just a little while longer.

because our God does not abandon His children. no matter what we've done.

we are His.

and He loves us.

and when you've made it through. and He's pulled you to the other side of your trial. look back on what you've learned and take it with you.

there's a reason why the rearview mirror is smaller than the windshield. we're meant to look back. not go back. if we're constantly looking back and driving forward, we're going to crash.

there's a difference between looking back on your mission and dwelling on it. look. don't dwell. remember it. don't lose sight of your future because you miss the past. take it with you. move forward. not on. and keep going forward. there is so much beauty ahead waiting for you.

and Christ is ahead too. waiting for you.

He was with you then. He is with you now. and He will be with you in the future too.

follow Him.

there is hope and healing ahead. in Him.

6 ::

we've talked about it earlier in this book. about opinions.

everyone. and I mean everyone. has an opinion. about everything. and everyone loves sharing their opinions on everything. ha I'm even doing it right now. with this book.

thing is, you can't listen to everyone and still follow Christ.

it just doesn't work that way.

simple. but super important.

people speak from their experiences. and that's okay. but what you have to understand is that there's not just one way to do things.

people are different. the gospel is the same.

remember that?

it's so true. and so important to remember. and to live by. what ties us together in a world of lots of people with lots of different experiences and lifestyles and opinions is one thing.

Jesus Christ.

so while it's good to listen to other people and accept advice and learn, there has to be a line.

you can't listen to everyone and still follow Christ.

His voice has to be your number one. not your mom's voice. or your dad's. not your friends'. or your bishop's. or your mission president's. it has to be God's. your Heavenly Father's. and your Savior. Jesus Christ's.

and you have to get to the point where what They say goes. period.

the way we learn to recognize Their voices is by following Them. coming to know Them. trusting Them. relying on Them. and building that relationship.

then you'll know Their voices. and you'll start to hear Their voices in others.

remember that divine filter? use it. every day. especially when it comes to taking advice from other people. see the good in their words. and pull from it. or don't.

let me be blunt about a pretty big mistake I see a lot of returned missionaries make. they come home. and they either feel or are told to believe that they are too inexperienced to just come home and start living their lives as adults.

they feel like they're too inexperienced with the "real world" to make competent, meaningful decisions for themselves. they question themselves. they doubt themselves. and they become sponges. soaking in everything they hear or are told, to the point where they don't hear themselves or the Lord anymore.

and they stop living.

now I'm not saying returned missionaries know everything. but they also haven't been living in some simplistic alternate reality for the past eighteen months or two years or however long they served for.

you were on your own out there. independent. making a conscious decision every single morning when you woke up to follow God. to do your best. to be happy. you motivated yourself. you were a disciple. you were a friend. a companion. an example. a leader.

that was you.

and then you came home.

and that should still be you.

you are not lost. you are not inexperienced. you are not naive. you are not confused.

you are a child of God who just gave Him a part of your life so that He could change you. mold you into the adult you are and will become.

so come home. stand on your own two feet. and live for Him.

don't let anyone tell you that you're capable of anything less. that you need help. that you "need" to be guided by your parents. or leaders. or others who have been home longer than you.

I've heard it so many times. that you weren't really independent because you were in the mission. you weren't really independent because you weren't living in the real world yet.

and I hate hearing that.

because it's not true.

and if God were standing here with you today, I can guarantee He wouldn't say that to you.

now let me be clear.

I'm not saying you should reject everyone's advice and take on the world by yourself.

no.

but I am saying that your opinion matters most. and so does God's.

so if something matters to you, do it. if you have a plan. follow it. if you don't, come up with one. stop doubting yourself. and don't take advice from people who would tear you down. or make you feel incapable.

God places people in our lives to help us. to guide us. you know the difference between right and wrong. between good and bad. and if the guidance you're receiving isn't leading you closer to God, then don't follow it.

doubt others before you doubt yourself.

you know how to make decisions. you were a leader. an example. a teacher. an adult choosing to follow God every day. you can do hard things. and you can make hard decisions.

you know enough.

especially when it comes to your own life.

out there, you were alone. yes you had support from home. but they weren't directly involved. you made your own decisions. and you learned independence. that's valuable. and something to be proud of you. something to hold on to.

God expects you to continue to learn and grow. from Him.

f r o m   H i m .

yes. he will send other people to teach you and support you. to guide and correct you.

but please don't ever think that your ability to receive revelation for yourself changes when you stand in the presence of someone who is more experienced than you are.

because it doesn't.

let me say that one more time.

your ability to receive revelation for yourself d o e s   n o t   c h a n g e when you stand in the presence of someone more experienced than you are.

that's not how it works.

personal revelation is communication between you and God. that's it. and what He has to say to you will always trump what someone else believes they have to say to you on His behalf.

you can hear advice from others without listening to it.

and you should.

you have not changed so much coming home that you can no longer think or decide things for yourself. you were capable of making decisions then. and you are capable of making them now.

you don't know everything. but you know enough.

and you definitely know enough to spot the difference between positive and negative advice.

the structure of my mission was solid. we worked very hard to never judge each other. we listened. we were taught to first govern ourselves. to take care of ourselves. and our decisions. to be smart. each missionary made his or her own decisions. and then they came together with their companions to decide together what to do next.

key word :: t o g e t h e r

in my mission you knew, no matter what, that someone always had your back. you just knew it. and you could count on it. you knew that you could speak your mind. respectfully. and you would be heard. respectfully. didn't matter if your opinion was popular or not. it was heard and respected. didn't matter if you had been a missionary for 16 months or for 16 days. your opinion was of equal importance. there was no hierarchy. there was no pecking order. because that's not how it works in the kingdom of God.

I am no better than someone who was just baptized. and I am no less than someone who holds a church leadership position. God doesn't love someone who goes to church every week more than someone who goes once a month or doesn't go at all.

that's just not how it works. we are all equal. that's how it was in the mission.

so why should that change when you come home?

it shouldn't.

you are in charge of yourself. you govern yourself. and then you come together with whoever it is in your life that you look to and respect for advice and opinions. and you should listen. respectfully. and you should be heard. respectfully.

the opinions of your parents and siblings and friends and leaders matter. they do. and I'm not trying to take anything away from them. they can guide you. and give solid advice for life trials that you and I have never seen or been through or even thought of before. they can be a resource and support system for you. so listen to them.

but don't ignore your own opinions and ideas and beliefs in the process.

the most important opinion in your life next to God's is your own.

yes.
your own.
your opinion matters. especially when it comes to your life. and your future.

God taught you how to make decisions by following His Spirit. so go make them. and trust your judgment.

you are a different person now than you were before you left to serve a mission. I can guarantee it. you've changed. so much in some areas. and maybe not so much in others. but you have changed. and you have the right to defend those changes. and you should.

think about it this way.

agency is a gift from God. your right to make your own decisions is a gift from God. and He sent His Son to die so that you and I could always have that right.

it's a gift. a sacred gift. and one that should be respected. always.

you see it every day on the mission. people using that sacred gift. if someone slammed a door in your face, you let them. and you walked on. if someone you were teaching suddenly stopped wanting to learn and asked you to leave, you did. and you walked on.

you respected their right to choose. knowing that God Himself gave them that right. and He respects their use of it. and so should you.

you learned to let people be who they are in that moment. to not box them in. to let them make decisions for themselves. about everything. you let them change. or not change. let them be exactly who they were and wanted to be. without loving them any less. and you respected them all the same.

you learned to accept and respect instead of expect.

and that is so important.

so when you stepped off the plane and walked into the arms of your family, you were different. you used your agency to make decisions for yourself. and to change.

and you need to defend those changes. respect yourself enough to accept the fact that you've changed. and keep living those changes.

don't come home and fall out of the tree and just lay there. embarrassed. don't go wander meaninglessly through the forest either. or be ashamed that you climbed a tree. or fell out of it. just get up. brush yourself off. and go climb another tree.

go find God again. and keep changing.

okay. we're going to switch audiences for a minute ::

I'm talking to the welcomers now. to the loving families who welcome home returned missionaries.

please. please. get to know your returned missionaries for who they are now. today. standing in front of you.

not who they were before they left. or who they were as a child. or a teenager. not who they were at their best. or their worst. or who you expect them to be.

your missionary has changed.

a c c e p t and r e s p e c t them . don't e x p e c t from them .

that is how you support a returned missionary. that is how you be a good welcomer. that is how you support your child. or brother. or sister. or cousin. or niece. or nephew. or friend. or that kid in your ward you've watched grow up since he was three. or that kid you just met.

there is no perfect returned missionary. I don't even know what that means. there's no cardboard cutout with a script. there's no requirements.

there are no expectations. or at least there shouldn't be.

but let me tell you what there are.

there are people. complex, individual people. young adults who have served God for an extended period of their lives. who have spent time with Him. been changed by Him. learned from Him. walked with Him.

and now they're home. and they just had all of that stripped away from them in one day.

they just had taken away from them one of the most sacred experiences they have ever lived. one of the most soul-touching. heart-wrenching. disciple-making experiences they have ever known and might ever know.

and whether they show it or not, that's hard. that is so hard. from one day to the next, their whole world shifts. without their consent. without warning, really.

and whether you see it or not. they're grieving.
they really are.

some returned missionaries that you meet will be happy to be home. some relieved. some excited. some anxious. some sad. some upset. some withdrawn. some depressed.

most returned missionaries you meet are going to be feeling all of that. constantly.

coming home from a mission is hard. so hard.

and to come home to expectations for school and marriage and career and whatever else there is to expect. that makes it harder.

and let's be honest. those expectations that you and I and all of the other welcomers seem to have for returned missionaries don't come from God.

they really don't.

because the only expectation that does come from God is simple. and clear.

follow Christ.

that's it.

f o l l o w   C h r i s t .

God doesn't expect them to come home and start college and get a degree.
that's you. and the other welcomers.

God doesn't have them on some timeline to get married before they "age out" or "expire."

that's you. and the other welcomers.

God doesn't expect them to take over the family business or focus on their careers before they miss some window.
that's you. and the other welcomers.

if God Himself respects their rights to decide who they are. and to change. why do we feel we get to disrespect those same rights? why do we feel we have the right to place expectations on a person God just spent so much time teaching and molding into his disciple?

we have no right.

He wants them to follow His Son. and find peace in Him. and be happy.

that's it.

and if you want to be a good welcomer, then that's what you should want for them too. support the changes that they have made within themselves. look past your expectations for them.

let go of the child you knew eighteen months ago or two years ago or however long they were gone for. and get to know the adult that just stepped off that plane in front of you.

because God changed them. and they need your support defending those changes now more than ever before. now more than ever they need to know that their earthly family can support the changes their Heavenly Father just made within them.

be a good welcomer.

as much as you loved the person they were before. let go of that. and love them now. that's all any of us need. to be loved. without expectations. to be respected and accepted and feel supported while we change and grow for ourselves.

so support them. love them. respect them. for who they a r e . not for who they w e r e .

nobody needs to be reminded of who they were. especially not when they've changed. or when they're trying to change. that never helps.

there's a reason why missionaries serve a w a y from their families. away from their homes. from their comfort zones. from familiarity.

and are sent somewhere completely different.

and I really think it's because He needs that time with them. one on One. to teach them things only a Heavenly Father can. about who they were. and really are. and who they can become.

He teaches them about discipleship. about His Son. our Brother. and what it means to follow Him. and that's what they do for eighteen months or two years or however long they serve for.

and He needs you to be a good welcomer. and just love them. respect the changes He has made within them. and support them. they need your support. they really truly do.

okay welcomers. let's talk about another huge pet peeve of mine.

probably the worst one of all. because it actually makes me angry.

stop making fun of our returned missionaries .

I'm serious.
just stop.

making fun of people or shaming people never did anyone any good. and it still doesn't do anyone any good. doesn't matter what the topic is. or what the situation is.

people don't want to be made fun of. or feel embarrassed. or out of place.

so stop.
and let it go.

we all know returned missionaries are socially awkward when they come home. it just happens. what do you honestly expect? they've been out teaching people about

God non-stop for the past eighteen months or two years or however long they served for. just God. 24 / 7 .

they've gone from a full schedule and a plan every day to tons of free time.

they aren't up to date on sports. or social media. pop culture. or music. they don't know how to just hang out. or chill. how to sit and watch a movie. they don't know how to talk to girls. or how to talk to guys. how to flirt. or have interests outside the gospel.

that just wasn't their world. for a good chunk time. it wasn't supposed to be.

they were s e t a p a r t from the world. remember? so they could teach people about Christ.

it will all come back to them with time. like riding a bike.

they'll get more comfortable. they will process their emotions. and their situations. and they'll move forward. in their time.

so let them. give them time.

just stop.
and let it go.

let them talk about their missions. that's all they knew for the whole time they were gone. and it meant a lot to them. more than you might comprehend.

we listen to each other tell stories all day. all the time. about trips. or vacations. or the good old days. about families. or friends. or petty drama. so why should mission stories be any different?

so stop.
and let it go.

let them come home. and figure things out.

we are children of God. living with and dealing with not just ordinary people. but other children of God. and He loves them. just as much as He loves you. He wants them to be happy. just as much as He wants you to be happy. He defends them. just like He would defend you. He grieves with them. just like He would grieve with you.

we are all children of God. so let's start acting like it. and treating each other like it.

because life is long. and beautiful. but hard. and no one should have to walk it alone.

we're all here to follow Christ.

and no one should have to follow Him alone.

or feel ashamed to talk about the experiences they've had following Him.

think about it this way. the power of b e i n g o n e is stronger than the power of o n e . being one creates a community so that no one has to walk alone.

the only One who had to walk alone was Jesus Christ. and even He didn't walk His whole journey alone. He was O n e with His Father and with the Holy Spirit.

His disciples came together to be o n e and follow Him together.

so should we.

we were placed in families. to be one. communities. to be one. countries. to be one. religions. to be one. to find unity. and to walk together. to follow Christ. together.

we can't even get back home by ourselves. we have to become o n e with God and Jesus Christ. we need to receive the gift of the Holy Spirit after baptism. so that He can guide us and be with us. and help us feel of God's love at all times. help us follow Christ.

that's why we are placed in wards. and stakes. why we go to Sacrament meeting. that's why religious groups of any denomination come together. not to be told how to worship. not to dictate how their relationship with God should be.

no.

but to provide a space. where people can come together. worship together. find Christ together. learn of Him together. and never. ever have to walk alone. so that we can be one.

in 1843 from jail, Joseph Smith wrote this ::

if it has been demonstrated that I have been willing to die for a "mormon," I am bold to declare before heaven that I am just as ready to die in defending the rights of a

Presbyterian, a Baptist, or of a good man of any denomination; for the same principle which would trample upon the rights of the latter-day saints would trample upon the rights of . . . any other denomination who may be unpopular and too weak to defend themselves (Smith, 1843).

being one doesn't mean we all think alike. doesn't mean we always agree. or believe the same. or live the same.

it means we stand together. by those we love. and by those we don't. and we defend each other. being one is having the same goal. not taking the same path to get to that goal.

in this case it is following Christ.

so if your returned missionary does things differently. values things differently. xyz I don't care whatever it is. let them. and follow Christ together.

lots of missions call their new missionaries "greenies." in my mission, we called them "oros." in spanish, *oro* means gold.

I remember that first day on my mission listening to my president talk about my particular group. there on our first day. not really knowing anything about anything. and he told us we were special. and sacred. and capable of so much. and it was because of the fact that we were brand new to the mission.

and I didn't get it.

I thought it was nice and all. but it didn't make sense to me until fifteen months later. I was sitting in a training the day before I was going to pick up my new companion. my first and only brand new missionary.

"do you know why the oros are so special?" our president asked us.

"because they're new" he said, "they don't know anything. they don't have anything. some of them don't even speak the language.

"but they have God. and they follow Christ.

"and that alone makes them capable of anything. and everything.

"these new elders and sisters are not going to learn as much from you as you will learn from them. and it is your responsibility to protect them. and to love them. and support them."

and it was true. my sweet companion loved God. with everything she had. and she was more committed to following Christ than to anything else.

she reminded me of who I had been fifteen months before. protected and shielded by my dear, earliest companions. who taught me. and respected me. who listened to me and always had my back. let me grow at my own pace and pushed me to follow Christ better.

and fifteen months later it was my chance to be that person for my sweet companion. to support her. and shield her. protect her. and respect her. to always have her back and to push her to follow Christ better.

but as our mission president promised. she taught me so much more than I ever taught her.

she taught me what it means to leave all and follow Christ. again. and again. and again. she lived intentionally. and made an effort to follow Christ. every day. something I was doing. but not as intentionally. not as well. not as deeply or with as much heart. and soul.

she woke that passion in me again. and my time with her was so sacred. and beautiful. and life-changing. and soul-stirring.

she reminded me that all we needed was God. that all we needed was to follow Christ. and everything would be okay. not easy. not without pain and sadness. but it would be okay. and we would become stronger for it.

she taught me so much. probably more than I ever taught her. and it was because of her dependence on God. and her decision to follow Him. intentionally. with her whole soul.

so to you. the families and the friends and the leaders of these returned missionaries.

to the welcomers ::

protect your oros. what they bring home with them is sacred. holy. it come directly from God. they have just come home from serving Him 24 / 7 . they need to be supported. and respected. loved. and listened to.

they have a lot to learn from you about life after the mission.

and you have a lot to learn from them about following Christ.

so learn from them.

let them remind you what it feels like to choose to follow Christ. intentionally. over and over and over again. let them wake that passion inside of you. guide you to Him. and recommit to living intentionally. and being better.

your returned missionaries have so much to offer.

it's not your job to change them. but to support them. not to lead them. but to walk with them. to be there for them. and let what they have to offer change you. and touch your heart.

we're all here together. following Christ. in our own ways.

we go to church to feel God's love. to strengthen each other. let's make it a safer space. a holy space. a space where we can find power. to overcome trials. to just keep walking. to care for one another. to raise children. to beat addictions. to repent. to stay positive. to trust. to learn. to believe. to thank. to forgive.

to follow Christ.

we're on this journey together.

the journey of discipleship.

7 ::

so this is it.

the rest of your life.

you're home from the mission. moving forward to another stage.

there are lots of stages to life. I think. I'm only twenty-six, so my experience is limited. but I know I've been through a few different stages already.

and through them all there was me. and there was Christ.

every day. every night. every job. every class. every new house or apartment. every ward. every everything I went through.

it was me and Him. and it still is. and it always will be.

follow Him. just follow Him.

recommit every day. all the time. whenever you think about it. and live intentionally. more intentionally than you did yesterday.

follow the peace. and the joy that comes with following Him. repent often. change often. and be happy. just be happy.

sometimes when I think about it, it's overwhelming. following Christ forever? being a disciple forever? I know I'm not perfect. I make mistakes. I have weaknesses. I get overwhelmed easily. I want to give up too often.

won't He just get tired of me?

I've asked God that question so many times. asking for forgiveness so that hopefully He doesn't get tired of me.

and then the Spirit comes.
and smacks me upside the head.

and I can feel God rolling His eyes at me.

because. that. is. not. how. things. work.

our God. our perfect Father. does not get tired of us.

we can't be "too imperfect" for Him. we don't get x amount of mistakes before He just lets us go or stops loving us.

God does not give up on us when we stop following Christ. or when we are too overwhelmed to even think straight.

that is not our God.

our God loves us. He loves you. and He loves me. and no matter what we do. or what we don't do. that love doesn't change. doesn't run out. doesn't leave.

you will always be good enough for God.

always.

it's non-negotiable.

He will never stop loving you. you are His child. and our God does not abandon His children.

ever.

I remember one sunday on my mission. I was playing the piano, the prelude music before Sacrament meeting started. we were watching and hoping the people we'd invited to come to church would show up. we'd worked hard that week. and invited a lot of people. I had a good feeling about it.

and none of them came.
not even one of them came.

I was so upset. and frustrated. and I kept playing it back through my head over and over during the Sacrament. I remember praying and asking God what we did wrong. we had worked so hard. we did our part. and none of those people came. why weren't our efforts good enough?

I felt like a failure. if I'd done my best and it still wasn't enough, then what was I even there for. why wasn't it working the way I'd wanted? the way we'd planned it?

and then the Lord corrected me. quietly. and gently.

reminding me that this was not my work. and I was not in charge here. that these were God's children. and He loved them. deeply. even though they didn't come. that He was working with them. He reminded me ever so gently that I was not the one guiding this work. but that I was just an instrument in His hands.

and I felt relief. just so much relief washing over me.

first :: because I realized that I couldn't mess up God's work. that me and my imperfections did not affect His work. it was and is H I S . and it will always be so much greater than you and me.

second :: because I learned my role. I am an instrument in His hands. I am His child. and He is grateful for my efforts and for yours. even when they're not perfect. even when we think that things aren't going according to plan. we have to remember that's our plan. not His.

His plan is deeper. holier. and is filled with so much love and respect and hope for His children. sometimes we can't comprehend it. and we don't always need to.

there is no right or wrong way to be a disciple. there is Christ. and following Him. that's it.

trust Him. have faith. and relax. don't worry so much. I have to remind myself of that so often. if you're following Christ, you're doing enough. period.

follow Him. with your heart. and your soul. live intentionally. the will of God and your agency are two beautiful, holy things that weave together to create your exaltation. you. yours. personalized to you. a beautiful reflection of your relationship with God. just you and Him.

I can guarantee He doesn't want us to spend all our time worrying that we're messing it all up because we're imperfect.

G o d k n o w s w e a r e i m p e r f e c t .

He knew we would be. that is why He sent His firstborn Son to die. for you. and for me. to right all of our wrongs. to protect us. and to give each of us the right to repent and change. over. and over. and over again.

that is our God. and He loves us. dearly.

all He asks is that we follow His Son. through all our stages.

you fell out of the tree when you came home. stand up. and move forward. keep walking. and get ready to fall over and over again. stop waiting for the fall. stop waiting for your mistakes to condemn you. stop waiting for everything to line up perfectly before you live.

go. now. follow your dreams. and live big. follow Christ.

stop waiting for the fall.

it will come. over and over and over again.

and Christ will be there to pick you up.

over and over and over again.

for the rest of your life.

that name tag may have come off your chest. but the discipleship was not meant to leave your soul. and it didn't. I know it didn't.

because as Elder Jeffrey R. Holland said, "after an encounter with the living Son of the living God, nothing is ever again to be as it was before" (Holland, 2012).

your situation will change. your stage of life will change. your job. your family role and dynamic. your friends. change is such a deep part of life. of eternity.

you will change. and if you follow Christ. those changes will bring you closer to Him.

I love the painting of Christ knocking at the door. the door with no handle. and I like to think what we would see through the door and on the other side.

we'd see a disciple of Christ. someone who walked with Him. who knew Him. someone He would come to visit. someone He would hope would answer. obviously so because He is knocking at the door. the door with no handle.

you and me are on the other side of the door. living our lives. day after day. going to work. and school. raising families. living our lives.

can you hear Him knocking?

with everything that's going on in your life and in mine.

can you hear Him knocking?

if you can. open the door. and let Him in. if you can't. open the door. and let Him in.

because I can guarantee He's standing there waiting.

make the necessary changes to be able to hear Him. quiet your life. talk to Him. ask Him questions. think of what He would say if He were here with you today.

keep Him near. and keep that door open.

you can't walk with a name tag on your chest anymore and represent Him like you did before. and you're not expected to anymore either. that was your calling. and you've since been released.

go live your life. follow Christ. and be happy.

and when He knocks. open the door.

you're a disciple of Christ.

when He knocks. open the door. when He asks you to testify of Him. open your heart and your mouth and testify. when He asks you to act. act. follow the promptings of the Holy Spirit. because that's Christ. speaking to you. that's Him knocking on the door.

live your life. and let Him live it with you.

follow Him.

always push yourself to become more like Him. follow Him. trust Him. take what you've learned and live it. take what you don't understand and learn about it. or let it go and trust Christ.

when we act on what we know, we begin to feel. and when we begin to feel, we understand more and more. that's conversion. it's an upward spiral. grow according to what you know. and let it lift you up. but don't let what you don't know stop you from living what you do know.

just like on the mission.

it's okay to say you don't know. and learn about it later.

God has said "stop, and stand still until I command thee, and I will provide means whereby thou mayest accomplish the thing which I have commanded thee" (*The Doctrine and Covenants.* 5:34).

why would God expect us to know the answers to everything before we could follow Christ? He wouldn't. and doesn't. so we shouldn't expect that from ourselves either. we trust what we know and we learn about what we don't know.

and we follow Christ.

night and day. through the good times and the bad.

we follow Christ.

I still have my backpack from the mission. I see it sitting there on my shelf sometimes. and it takes me back. reminds me. it was with me. in the rain. in the cold. in the heat. when I was happy. or sad. healthy. or sick. it was there. on my back. every day. all day.

it's faded brown. the straps are worn. the zippers don't hardly work. there's a huge hole in the top. I didn't even have to use the zippers for the last half of my mission. the hole was so big I could just reach in and out. but it walked with me. the entire time.

a silent reminder of the other One who walked with me. the whole time. every single step.

my Savior. Jesus Christ.

He walked with me. through the rain. and the cold. the heat. when I was happy. or sad. healthy. or sick. He was there. by my side. every day. all day.

He was there. He saw it. felt it. lived it. He loved me. made me strong. made me who
I am. and continues to love me. and make me who I am. I love Him. and am forever in His debt.

He still walks with me. and with you. everywhere. every day. all day. asking us to follow Him. to trust Him. don't let what you don't know about the gospel stand in the way of what you do know about your Savior.

we are here to follow Him. Jesus Christ.

God knows your heart. He created you. after His own likeness and image. there is no one like you. He made you different because He needs you to be different. He knows you.

and you are His.

I remember Uruguay like it was yesterday. and I miss it. more than I can even explain. so. so. deeply. I miss walking those streets. sitting in those houses. meeting people. introducing people to their Savior. watching the tears fall down their faces as they felt His love. some of them for the first time ever. others for the first time in years.

I can't be there anymore. I can't wipe their tears. or hold them in my arms. I can't see them smile or watch them weep as they feel the love of God touch their hearts. change them. I can't watch them change for Him. see the conversion burning in their eyes. in their souls.

I can't feel that rain fall on my face. or walk up and down those hills. I can't feel the tired ache in my legs and feet. or wake up knowing the whole day was going to God.

I will never feel a lot of those things again. because I came home. and it ended.

but I came to know my Savior Jesus Christ. all He went through. all He sacrificed. He who walks with us still. I came to know the nature of my God. our Father. the Creator of all. who knows our names. who loves us. deeply.

it was me and Him. and He changed me.

those were some of the most sacred years of my life. because they were His. I gave them to Him.

I left my mission. but my Savior never left me.

you left your mission. but your Savior never let you.

so now I'm here. at home. I have a job. I've gone to school. I have parents. and siblings. I pay rent. I have debt. I have friends. and a happy life. I have tears and pain. sorrow and joy. happiness and laughter.

sometimes I have things figured out. and other times I have no idea what's going on.

but through it all. I have Him.
just like I had Him in Uruguay.

in my life.
in my heart.
in my home.
in my words.
in my actions.
in all that I am.
in my thoughts.
in my very being.

He is here. because I still follow Him.

to those returned missionaries who have come home and left the path.

I know how it is to serve a mission. I went. I served. I came home. and I cannot deny the divinity and holiness of the work we were called to do.

it is the work of God Himself. the work of salvation. and there is nothing more beautiful and eternal than that special work.

I know how it feels to sit in a lesson with someone who doesn't understand. or doesn't want to.

I know how it feels to sit in front of someone who is struggling to find peace. and answers. and revelation. but who won't accept Christ as their Savior and solution.

I've sat in homes and held hands of people who were terrified to take the next step. who felt they were unworthy of God's love. people who had lost hope.

I've cried with mothers who had lost their children to the world. cried with spouses who didn't know what to do as they watched their families fall apart.

I've sat in homes and seen faces light up with an inexpressible joy. the joy that comes ONLY.

and I repeat ::

O N L Y

when one realizes that one has a Savior.

when one realizes that there is Someone who understands. Someone who knows them. the beautiful and the ugly parts of them. and still loves them. and will never leave them.

I know how it feels to see someone change their life because they finally understand and remember why they are here.

I know how it feels.

and so do you.

God changed me. and He changed you too. He loves me. and He loves you too. I wore that tag and carried His name. and you did too.

coming home is hard.
following Christ is hard.

I get it. I know it. I feel it.

but that is not reason enough to forsake our Savior.

I am not here to judge. Lord knows we all have sins. and mistakes. I have mine just like you have yours. some are visible. some aren't. I'm no better than you. and you're no better than me.

but don't leave. please don't leave.

your Savior loves you. knows your name. knows your heart. and is willing to sit with you through it all. let Him love you. let Him in.

and please come back.

the mission wasn't a box you checked. you didn't "do enough" for God to coast for a few years. it wasn't some spiritual high that left you with a post-mission hangover.

it was a beautiful. sacred experience. a gift from God to teach you one thing.

and one thing only.

by now I hope I don't even have to say it.

the mission was to teach you how to follow Christ.

to follow Christ. and be happy.

that's why we're here. that's why Christ gave His life. that's why we should be doing everything we do in the church. that's why we believe everything we believe. because it will help us follow Christ and be happy.

so you fell out of the tree.

get up.
keep walking.
go climb another tree.

and don't wait for the next fall.

know that God will pick you up. every. single. time.

you've got this.

my absolute favorite story in the Book of Mormon is about the three nephites.

before Christ left the nephites for the last time, to go back up to heaven, he asked his twelve disciples what they wanted from Him.

nine of the disciples wanted to live long lives and then come home to the presence of God and rest. it was given to them. the other three disciples wanted to stay on the earth. and preach and testify of Christ until He came again. it was also given to them.

the three disciples felt ashamed for what they wanted from Christ. ashamed. even though they knew as we also know :: that shame doesn't come from God.

but Christ was quick to correct them. He called them blessed. because He saw their hearts :: they wanted to serve Him. until the very end.

see the three nephites could have ended it then and there. they could have lived long, good lives. and then gone to heaven. just like the other nine disciples.

but they chose more.
they chose to stay.
and to follow Christ. forever.

until God Himself took them off the earth and told them it was time to rest.

see the difference?

both groups of disciples were wonderful missionaries. they both loved God. they both served Him. they both followed Christ.

but the second group chose to follow Christ for e t e r n i t y .

they chose to serve Him until H E called them home. not until their time ended.

we get to choose. if we will follow Christ for two years. or for eternity. if we will serve until our time is done. or if we will serve until He calls us home.

in my absolute favorite talk of all time, Elder Jeffrey R. Holland said ::

to all within the sound of my voice, the voice of Christ comes ringing down through the halls of time, asking each one of us while there is time, "do you love me" . . . and if at such a moment we can stammer out, "yea, Lord, thou knowest that I love thee," then

He may remind us that the crowning characteristic of love is always loyalty. (Holland, 2012).

the crowning characteristic of love is always l o y a l t y .

loyalty to Christ. loyalty to Him.

following Him to the end of our days. and on from then until He tells us to rest.

loyalty. it is an eternal commitment.

a commitment to be happy.
a commitment to change. constantly.
a commitment to follow Christ to the end.
a commitment to get up every time we fall out of the tree. brush off. and go climb another tree.

so go. follow Christ. and live intentionally.

hoy es el día.

vívalo.

hoy. mañana. y para siempre.

today is the day.

live it.

today. tomorrow. and forever.

and choose to follow Jesus Christ.

forever.

so go be His.

works cited ::

The Bible. Authorized King James Version, Intellectual Reserve Inc, 1979.

The Book of Mormon: Another Testament of Jesus Christ. Intellectual Reserve Inc, 1981.

The Pearl of Great Price. Intellectual Reserve Inc, 1981.

The Doctrine and Covenants. Intellectual Reserve Inc, 1981.

Holland, Jeffrey R. "'Lord, I Believe.'" *The Church of Jesus Christ of Latter-Day Saints.* Apr. 2013. www.lds.org/general-conference/2013/04/lord-i-believe?lang=eng.

Holland, Jeffrey R. "Tomorrow the Lord Will Do Wonders among You." *The Church of Jesus Christ of Latter-Day Saints.* Apr. 2016. www.lds.org/general-conference/2016/04/tomorrow-the-lord-will-do-wonders-among-you?lang=eng.

Holland, Jeffrey R. "The First Great Commandment." *The Church of Jesus Christ of Latter-Day Saints.* Oct. 2012. www.lds.org/general-conference/2012/10/the-first-great-commandment?lang=eng.

Monson, Thomas S. "The Will Within." *The Church of Jesus Christ of Latter-Day Saints.* Apr. 1987. www.lds.org/general-conference/1987/04/the-will-within?lang=eng.

Nelson, Russell M. "Revelation for the Church, Revelation for Our Lives." *The Church of Jesus Christ of Latter-Day Saints.* Apr. 2018. www.lds.org/general-conference/2018/04/revelation-for-the-church-revelation-for-our-lives?lang=eng.

Smith, Joseph. "The Prophet's Legacy." *The Church of Jesus Christ of Latter-Day Saints.* 1843.https://history.churchofjesuschrist.org/content/the-prophets-legacy?lang=eng

Uchtdorf, Dieter F. "The Way of the Disciple." *The Church of Jesus Christ of Latter-Day Saints.* Apr. 2009. www.lds.org/general-conference/2009/04/the-way-of-the-disciple?lang=eng.

Made in the USA
Las Vegas, NV
09 February 2022